CRUCIAL
CONVERSATIONS

BRIDGING THE AWKWARD SPIRITUAL GAP

amazonkindle
kindle publishing

CRUCIAL CONVERSATIONS

Kindle Publishing KDP, Seattle WA
kdp.amazon.com
Copyright © 2017 by Dan Grider. All rights reserved.
First Edition

The Crucial Questions are adapted from
Irresistible Evangelism, Natural Ways to Open Other to Jesus. Steve Sjogren, Dave Ping, Doug Pollock. 2004 &
God Space, Where Spiritual Conversations Happen Naturally, Doug Pollock, Group Publishing, Loveland CO 2009

Scripture taken from the New International Version®, Copyright © 1973, 1978, 1984 Bible Publishers. Used by permission of Zondervan Bible Publishers.

ISBN: 978-0-9990797-06

Cover Design: Chase Grider Tyler Goode
Line Editing: Tara Frost, Debbie Grider Beck & Dan Reminenschneider
Copy Editing: Rodney Arnold, Josh Duncan,
General Editor: Norman Jameson

CONVERSATIONS ₂

TABLE OF CONTENTS

Introduction: page 4
Section One: Crucial Conversations
Change How We Relate   **page 14**
Chapter 1 The Bridge   page 16

Chapter 2 The Principle of the 42's   page 36

Section Two: Crucial Conversations
Changing How Tell Our Story   **page 62**
Chapter 3 Crucial Conversations About a Life Change Story   page 64

Chapter 4 Basic Mistakes Telling Our Story   page 74

Section Three: Crucial Conversations
Change How we Connect With People   **page 96**
Chapter 5 Crucial conversations With a Cultural Believer   page 98

Chapter 6 Crucial Conversations with Christian (*!@#-) page 114

Chapter 7 Crucial Conversations, The Power of Pisteuo   page 130

Section Four: Crucial Conversations
Change How We Think   **page 150**
Chapter 8 Crucial Conversations About a New Life   page 152

Chapter 9 Conversations, Asking Innocent Awe Questions page 168

Section Five: Crucial Conversations
Change How we Approach People   **page 186**
Chapter 10 Conversations With a Down And Outer   page 188

Chapter 11 Crucial Conversations Not Evangelistic Presentations   page 206

Section Six: Crucial Conversations
Changes How We Disciple   **page 228**
Chapter 12 Crucial Conversation With Jesus First Disciple   page 230
Appendix A   page 240

I dedicate this book to Tiffany and Chase. As California Kids, you have had to translate the Gospel to your secular friends on a daily basis. Thank you for giving me the daily lessons in secular translation. You are the best. I love how you love Jesus, and how you love each other. Keep on speaking Jesus, to those who aren't yet fluent in Jesus. Thank you for all that you have taught me, and continue to teach me.

I love you both
Dad

INTRODUCTION

A thick cloud of fog rose as the cool coastal breeze clashed with the warm San Francisco air in the early morning of May 27, 1937. The first commuter was just rolling across the newly constructed Golden Gate Bridge on his way to work on the other side of the bay.

This bridge would become one of the most easily recognized structures in the world. For thirty years it was the longest suspension bridge in the world, leading engineers to declare it one of the wonders of the modern world. In 1918, nearly twenty years before that first car would utilize the modern marvel, research began to determine how to span the icy torrent that flowed through the Golden Gate Strait. How could San Francisco residents connect to the northern shore of Marin County?

Eventually, construction of the 1.7 mile long bridge

required more than 80,000 miles of wire. Each cable hanging from the 746-foot tall support structures had 27,000 strands. Its 16,750 workers applied more than 1.2 million rivets and poured 352,300 cubic yards of concrete to conquer the gulf and create the span now utilized by 10,000 cars per day.

All told, it took four years and four months of grueling labor to accomplish what must have seemed an impossible task.

That is a lot of sacrifice, trouble and expense for a single bridge, especially since eleven men gave their lives to build it. But throughout history, people have willingly bent to such enormous tasks to build connections.

Something inside of us makes us want to connect with others. It is in our DNA. Our Heavenly Father placed a drive within us that will not allow us to ignore chasms that separate us. It was the Father himself who took the greatest step to bridge the widest expanse – the gulf that separated us from Him.

The image of a bridge is the best picture for why we should have **crucial conversations**. The concept of a bridge is central to everything Jesus did while He was on earth. He saw the divide that had been created by sin.

"The original bridge builder was God the Father"

He knew that he had to personally become the bridge so we could know and have a relationship with the Father.

THE RELATIONAL DIVIDE
REQUIRES A BRIDGE

The divide that separated us demanded that the Heavenly Father build bridges to reach those far from Him, and leave us a model for constructing conversations that would do the same. Fundamentally, we are to reproduce what He has done for us. We reflect the heart of the Father when we reach across the divide. Refusing to do so makes us irrelevant in Kingdom work and the life giving Gospel message will lose credibility in our culture.

Why? Because at some level the secular world is capable of bridging the divide better than we are. Nonbelievers have co-opted the heartbeat of the Christian message of forgiveness, compassion, and second chances. How did this get flipped? Time is running out. We must not delay getting back to our primary mission. We are to reflect the heart of our Father and build a bridge across the divide.

Crucial conversations occur when we:

1. BUILD RELATIONAL BRIDGES

The primary mission of Jesus was to bridge the chasm that separates creation from its creator. He gave us a similar assignment, commissioning us to engage a lost world in a conversation that will lead to life and hope, not just for this life, but for all eternity. Jesus draws us in as co-engineers in closing the relational divide. His last words on earth were an assignment to all who would take up their cross and follow Him. This bridge building assignment is a call to "make disciples." And it's not just for a select few, either. We are called to take this bridge motif to all people – connecting them with the Father.

THE RELATIONAL DIVIDE

We don't have to be intimidated by the differences we see in other people. It doesn't matter if you think xenophobia, homo-phobia, and an ever-increasing list of phobias are on the rise. We are commissioned to be different. We have been equipped by the Holy Spirit to bridge this divide. We are to share and live beyond race, gender, culture or politics. We can do that – and become more like Jesus in the process – when we equip ourselves for crucial conversations. When you embrace the skills that Jesus modeled you will become a bridge builder who will span divides instead of broadening them.

Jesus' mission is most affirmed when wanderers find their way home. And while Jesus was on earth, He knew the best way to lead them home was to find them where they live, relate to them as they are, and then walk by their side, stride by stride, toward the Father.

When the Spirit of God reshapes your heart He will move you to love those who struggle and not to be threatened by those who succeed. He will give you the ability to connect with both the insiders and the outcast; with those who are just like you and with those who are worlds apart.

The fact that the Father built a bridge to you has to stir your heart to step across the discomfort of what may seem impossible to connect with someone on the other shore. When we are in touch with the amazing work of Jesus we will work to span the gulf for the person the Holy Spirit has placed on your heart. He will strengthen your span to make the connection, and in doing so, you will find the differences

"When we join people in their journey, they can't help but warm up to us, and the gospel message"

of those on the opposite shore actually will be the very thing that stimulates you to grow in your relationship with the Father.

When you meet people in everyday conversations, do you think about building bridges? Or do you remain comfortable in the status quo? Are you available to do the work of the Holy Spirit in this area? Have you actively thought about how you can better understand those who are different from you?

Building bridges is really about taking a step. Whether your first step is large or small, just take it to start building the bridge to span whatever gulf separates you. In mid stride, you will discover that something has happened to your heart. Somehow Christ has become more fully formed in you.

This book is titled *Crucial Conversations* because the only resource a Christ-less world has for knowing the Father's life saving message is for people who know Him to hold crucial conversation with those who do not.

Through these conversations, you and I build the bridge the Father will use to connect more of His children to Himself. Research proves this. Almost everyone who steps across the threshold of faith did so because of a crucial conversation. They may have taken a public step of faith, but behind the scenes was undoubtedly a Christ follower who engaged them in a conversation that in some way led to their decision.

The Father has enlisted you and I in the miracle of bridge building. He has allowed us to live, work, and play among myriads of people whom He is longing to reach. You and I must learn how to build a bridge to them by learning how to have effective, crucial conversations. The span between Christian and secular is widening at a shocking pace. We must understand and become students who learn how to reach across the relational divide. We must become the bridge that spans the chasm.

"We get to participate in the single greatest assignment ever given"

CONVERSATIONS THAT REACH ACROSS THE DIVIDE

In this book, you will learn how to identify potential spiritual conversations, and explore how to engage and develop them when opportunity arises. Living as if on mission will create the drive we need to engage our lost friends in crucial conversations.

2 LIVE INTENTIONALLY ON MISSION

You are reading this book because you have probably had the transformative work of Christ occur in your life and you want to help others have the same life changing experience.

For me, He seemed to give a passion gear in my transmission that wasn't there before. When you have been redeemed and restored by the Father your gear for relating to others shifts. I had a new desire to see others embrace the same hope and joy I had. I wished for them to see life from an eternal perspective instead of from their temporal, hopeless vantage point. I desired that all people come to know God as Father, not just some distant, uncaring Deity in the clouds.

Penn Jillette, a performer and author who is half of the Penn and Teller magic duo, is known for his atheistic rants. One of them caught my eye on YouTube recently. He described a man who approached him after a show. After a few moments of polite conversation, the guy gave him a Bible with a note in it. The man had taken the time to write a non-judgmental note that was thoughtful and loving. Surprisingly, Jillette was appreciative of this encounter, and the relational way someone cared enough about him to share his beliefs with him.

Jillette's conclusion was, "if Hell is real why don't more Christians act like they believe it? This guy really believed I am going to Hell." He posed the question, "If you believe it's real what would you do to keep someone you care about from going there?"

"Living on mission doesn't happen accidentally - it is a life investment."

He illustrated it this way, "If a truck was barreling down on someone you loved, and they did not see it coming, what would you do to shove them out of harm's way? You would do whatever's necessary" His conclusion was most Christians must not believe that Hell is real. If they did, wouldn't they have these crucial conversations?

3. LEARN HOW TO ASK GOOD QUESTIONS

Jesus was intentional about how he engaged people in conversation. His first words almost always formed a question. We almost always start with an invitation to a church event or a doctrinal statement. Virtually every time Jesus spoke, He began by learning where the other person was. His simple questions tested the waters to see if they were willing to keep talking.

If someone was rude to or resisted Jesus He didn't come back hard or say something cutting. He often responded with a question. We can learn from His approach. By asking an appropriate question he could respond without becoming adversarial. It also allowed Him to test their spiritual openness.

Jesus didn't air drop deep spiritual diatribes on his potential conversationalists. He'd ask a thought-provoking question and then **listen** to the answer to tell him what direction He should take in the conversation.

We can all develop the skill of asking good questions and listening. We will explore in each chapter how we can better learn to ask people thought-provoking questions that will lead to deeper conversations. The tool box section will provide suggestions for the kind of questions you can ask when you have crucial conversations.

4. TELLING YOUR STORY

Most of us have not developed the art of sharing our testimony. We may never be the person prompted to "tell that story again…" We may never receive our 15 minutes of fame.

You, however, have a story that must be told, a bridge that must be built. What Christ follower could possibly have nothing important to say or be leading a boring life? You need to learn that no matter how ordinary you think you life, your story becomes interesting when you learn how to tell it.

You're not a boring person. Don't let that lie make you hesitate to share your story. Still, telling our stories has nothing to do with being exciting or boring. There is a skill involved you can learn to develop.

The power of your story is that God – the creator of the universe, and all that is seen and unseen – has engaged Himself in your life. Because of that you are not who you once were.

Remember to keep the focus of your story on the work of the Father. He is at work in you, and desires to be the story in your life everyday that you live. We will discuss later how to cultivate this perspective when we talk about developing the skills to better tell your story in light of the broader gospel story.

The art of this skill is that God will merge what you read in the scriptures with an example from your current life. The key is to learn to see how those two elements fit together. The intersection of your life and the Scriptures makes your story powerful. This skill will also ignite in you a new hunger for consuming the scripture.

Every Christ follower possesses two types of stories or testimonies. You have a life change story, which tells of your original Christ encounter. Your other story is telling about how the Father provides on a daily basis. When Christ followers hear the term "testimony" they usually think of the life change story. That's why the testimony offered by older adults can seem ancient and irrelevant.

Expand your definition of story/testimony beyond the details surrounding conversion. Make it current. Learning to adapt your story can be a powerful tool to open spiritual conversations. Most of us have not been taught how to share our story. We must learn to listen to the Holy Spirit and find appropriate opportunities to connect with the other person.

When these newly developed skills meet the hunger produced by the Spirit of God in your life, the conversations you have every day will be transformed to mimic those found throughout the New Testament. But these aren't just normal, mundane conversations.

These are crucial conversations.

crucial

CHANGE

How we relate

conversations

SECTION 1

STORY OF A HARDENED MAN
ZACCHAEUS LUKE 19:2-9

Luke 19:2-4 A man was there by the name of Zacchaeus; he was a chief tax collector and was wealthy. He wanted to see who Jesus was, but because he was short he could not see over the crowd. So he ran ahead and climbed a sycamore-fig tree to see him, since Jesus was coming that way.

Luke 19:5 When Jesus reached the spot, he looked up and said to him, "Zacchaeus, come down immediately. I must stay at your house today." So he came down at once and welcomed him gladly.

Luke 19:7 All the people saw this and began to mutter, "He has gone to be the guest of a sinner." But Zacchaeus stood up and said to the Lord, "Look, Lord! Here and now I give half of my possessions to the poor, and if I have cheated anybody out of anything, I will pay back four times the amount.

Luke 19:9 Jesus said to him, "Today salvation has come to this house, because this man, too, is a son of Abraham. For the Son of Man came to seek and to save the lost.

"If you get an amazing opportunity but you are not sure you can do it, say yes – work out the details later!"
— **Richard Branson**

"Look for opportunities in all circumstances...refuse to be passive."
— **Lailah Gifty Akita**

CHAPTER 1

THE BRIDGE

Recently the rate of cyclists injured in accidents involving automobiles was soaring in London. The Transportation for London Board (TFL) produced an ad campaign that has become an international sensation. The campaign, called "The Awareness Test," features two teams of basketball players, one dressed in black and the other in white. The voice over announcer asks in a thick British accent, "How many passes does the team in white make?" Then the video plays of two teams rapidly passing the ball among themselves.

Most people are concentrating on counting the passes, and are pleased when they get the number correct. It was 13. But the announcer asks a second, more important question – "Did you see the moon walking bear?"

Concentrating on the obvious element to watch, no viewers saw a moon walking bear. No one was looking for, or expected to see, a moon walking bear. The video is rewound and replayed a second time, and sure enough there it is – a moon walking bear.

The ad pointed out to motorists how easy it is to miss a cyclist if they aren't looking for one.

The point is self-evident. We don't see things for which we aren't looking. People didn't notice a bear dancing like Michael Jackson because they were carefully counting the passes. I have shown it to hundreds of people, and never has anyone seen the bear the first time.

The moon walking bear represents the vast numbers of people we encounter every day who are spiritually open and hungry. Yet we pass them by because we aren't looking for them and don't see them. These are our friends, co-workers, neighbors, and even church members who don't know how to find answers to the gnawing pain inside them. They aren't even aware that their affliction is spiritually sourced. They long to discuss their condition, but they don't know where to turn, who to ask, or how even to bring it up.

John Lennon once said, "Life is what happens to you while you're busy making other plans." Most of the people we pass every day are doing all that they know to do. They don't intend to become spiritually hardened. They don't intend to live separated from the Father. They are just going through the paces of life. Most of their days look alike. They're anesthetized by the cadence of their existence. They plan to deal with the big questions of life, they just haven't gotten around to it yet.

CRUCIAL CONVERSATION WITH A SPIRITUALLY HARDENED MAN

CONVERSATIONS
Bridge To Zaccahaeus

Jesus was on His way to the most important appointment of His life. He was heading toward the eternally significant appointment to redeem all humankind. He was making His final ascent to Jerusalem where He would be crucified.

He could have been preoccupied with the salvation of the world. He could have been consumed with the heinous death that lurked just hours away. He could have been throwing a pity party for himself, but He wasn't. He remained alert to the possibility of connecting with others on His way.

He glimpsed a man no one in the crowd noticed, a small, rich guy in a tree. Rich guys in that day were almost always reviled, Roman tax collectors. A rich man clinging to a tree branch

"Jesus made a point to always be about his Father's business"

would likely be a tax collector, because other wealthy men would have a posse to clear their way. Not tax collectors. They lived solitary lives, and Zaccahaeus would have been no different. He had undoubtedly prospered by feeding off of the helpless plight of the poor. He would have collected whatever "tax" he wanted above the quota demanded by the Romans because he had the might of Rome behind him.

Now Jesus, on His way to the cross, not only spotted Zaccahaeus but made a detour into the house of this hardened man. No one could do the job of collecting taxes for the occupying Roman government unless he had become calloused to the pain of his own friends and neighbors. Zaccahaeus created a posh life for himself at their expense. All his possessions didn't reduce the expanse of the divide he felt in his soul.

Jesus paused long enough to see if He could build a bridge to a man most people would curse under their breath and take the long way around to avoid. Jesus saw the divide that separated Zaccahaeus from him and the Father. We hear only a portion of their conversation, but we know a few things about Jesus. He probably asked Zaccahaeus some penetrating questions, and showed him that the path he was on did not have to be the road of his future.

After Zaccahaeus dined with Jesus, everything changed. On the other side of that meal, Zacchaeus declared that the possibility of new life had shaken him to the core. He no longer needed to trust in his bank account. He transferred his trust to Jesus.

To show how this trust transfer worked, he volunteered to give a majority of his resources to the poor people he had defrauded. Jesus built a bridge to a hardened man's heart. Building bridges takes time, effort, and sensitivity. Jesus was alert and open to developing a crucial conversation.

This encounter changed Zacchaeus' life and eternity. I will bet that after that his story might go something like this:

"I had lost perspective on life. When someone would ask me, 'How much is enough?' I would say, 'A little bit more.' Whatever I had never was enough. My whole life was wrapped up in what I owned. My possessions perverted everything, every relationship, every conversation, every thought."

"Then one day a man came riding through town shouting that Jesus was headed our way. Hearing that shot a lightening bolt through my body. I had to see him. I was dying on the inside. I had no idea what to do, so I climbed on a low hanging branch to catch a glimpse."

"It was like Jesus knew I had a hole in my heart. I didn't know how to ask for what I needed, but He seemed to know my needs better than I did. By the end of the evening it was like I had a new chariot driver. I knew I had to let go of the reins and trust them to His hand."

We never know the dramatic impact on a life when we build a bridge to them. The person who is separated from Christ doesn't know how to build the bridge to the Father or know how to ask us relevant questions. We know how this feels because we were once on the bank of Christ-less desperation.

It is easy to become like Zacchaeus, hardened by years of futile attempts to find meaning and purpose; hardened by layers of cynicism and skepticism grown over our once supple heart; hardened because of culture that ignores and even prospers at the expense of people in pain. There he was perched in a tree, looking, hoping for something to assuage his personal emptiness. Hardened people are empty, hurting people.

Have you ever noticed that the best opportunities happen at the most inopportune times? Like Jesus spotting Zaccahaeus on his way to an incredibly important appointment. These opportunities seem to come when we are busy, in the midst of important work. But Jesus illustrated that nothing important happens if we never make the effort to build the bridge.

THE CASE OF NO BRIDGE

THE NEED FOR Bridge Building: Close friends Justin and Natalie were traveling back to her hometown following news of her brother being in a serious motorcycle accident. Natalie had been raised in a good home. They even went to church occasionally, but her family showed no signs of real spiritual life so they had been praying about how to share their newfound faith in Jesus with her family. They decided they would move the conversation toward Jesus on this trip.

Are Justin and Natalie like us? We see those we love as good people, but they seem to be living far from Jesus. As Justin and Natalie drove, they discussed how they were going to share their faith, a step that should be simple but seemed so daunting. They found themselves repeating, "We wish we'd had some preparation or training for how to do this."

They had taken recently an evangelism training class that gave them a set of memorized verses and practiced conversations to lead a person through the steps of praying the sinner's prayer. But nothing trained them in natural ways to listen for clues that a person was spiritually open to a crucial, spiritual conversation.

The training was one sided, preparing them to deliver a message, but not to listen to a person's heart hunger. It had prepared them to lead a conversation toward a predetermined result.

They longed for a session on how to look for natural ways to identify an opening for a spiritual conversation so they didn't feel like a spiritual time-share sales person. Their training seemed irrelevant as they talked with each other about how they were going to engage their family members in this most crucial conversation.

"How do you have a vibrant, first step spiritual conversation?" they asked each other. Their question provided the motivation for this book.

When they arrived home they were relieved that Dustin, Natalie's brother, had emerged from surgery and the prognosis was much better than they had feared. It appeared there would be some post-surgery rehab time, but he would make a full recovery.

Natalie suggested the family offer a prayer of thanks to the Father for Dustin's successful surgery. The nine family members huddled in the surgical waiting room breathed a grateful sigh of relief and agreed to hold hands and pray. As Natalie led, she prayed that this would provide the impetus for Dustin to open his life to Jesus and take the next step toward surrendering his life to Christ.

As she finished her prayer, her mom – matter of factly said, "Honey, Dustin is going to heaven. He prayed the prayer and was baptized when he was eight."

This seemed to be the opening for which Natalie hoped. Unfortunately, while she seized the opportunity to launch a conversation, she skipped the important first step of building a bridge. She didn't lay the foundation by simply sharing a brief story of what had recently happened to her. Her spiritual eyes had been opened to a new way of seeing the world. She had recently had a transformative experience with her Heavenly Father, ever since she had hopes of later following up with her mom and family.

Instead, Natalie did what so many eager Christians revert to in those same situations. Natalie began to preach.

To the same nine people she had just led in prayer, Natalie declared that Dustin obviously hadn't surrendered his life to Christ. Never once since his eight-year-old obligatory "church response" had he shown any indication that he wanted to follow Jesus. She pointed out that he was simply responding to the pressure that their mom had laid on him to do the "church thing." She ended by lobbing a rhetorical grenade that rocked the room.

"Mom, have you ever noticed that Dustin is hardened spiritually and calls himself an atheist?"

Her mom collapsed in tears. The rest of the family pierced her with disapproving, steely glares. In that moment motivated by innocent passion for the eternal soul of a brother she loved, Natalie realized something. Her entire family was just as hardened as Dustin.

Her approach assumed that her mom and siblings understood how essential it was for Dustin to soften his heart toward Jesus. She failed to realize that every member of her family had become spiritually hardened. They didn't know what authentic life transformation looked like.

Mortified, Natalie suddenly realized her assumptions were wrong, her timing was wrong, and her approach was wrong. She had blurted out way more than she could unpack there.

Yes, she had voiced something everyone already knew – that Dustin had become spiritually resistant. Inadvertently, she had condemned them in her observations about Dustin. She didn't realize her condemning, judgmental tone would alienate everyone in her family. Any bridge she had hoped to build had just been set on fire by her verbal grenade. Hoping to salvage the moment, her sister responded, "Let's just agree to make all religious views off limits for this family. Ok? End of story."

Just like that, the bridge to her family had been burned to the ground. Justin and Natalie had done the very thing they had feared. They had offended her family without ever sharing the hope they have in Christ. Every family member had become a bit more vulnerable that day because of what had just happened to Dustin. Natalie's innocent blunder shut the conversation down for years to come.

On the return trip home, Justin and Natalie evaluated what had happened in the hospital waiting room. "All I did was pray for Dustin's salvation," Natalie said. "Can't they see his spiritual condition? We almost lost him today." Justin cautiously reminded her of what had actually transpired. He reminded Nathalie that she had shared more than a prayer. The prayer alone could have produced spiritual conversations. While she had properly assessed their spiritual need, she shared a spiritual truth at a time and in a way that the family members couldn't receive. She had failed to initiate any positive spiritual conversation, and instead erected a wall. Her sister put a moratorium on spiritual conversation moving forward. Natalie's

"Avoid pre-deciding to have a spiritual conversation…let the process happen naturally"

spiritual passion produced nothing more than hurt feelings and a resolve on both sides to avoid vital, eternal topics.

While Natalie's intentions were good, she went wrong where so many go wrong – her timing couldn't have been worse. Dustin's accident had the family emotionally frazzled. Timing was Natalie's own biggest foe as she let her emotions drive the conversation, pre-deciding on this course while on the way to the hospital.

That decision – pre-deciding that a crucial conversation will take place before a door opens – will always result in an awkward, forced conversation. We must learn the skill of looking for natural spiritual openings, and learn how to engage others naturally at the appropriate time. When we learn this skill we will discover that others provide the bridge to spiritual topics all the time.

Choosing the large group setting guaranteed that Natalie's comments would not prompt positive spiritual conversations, but rather would start a negative group process. At no point did she share her personal story or learn what any individual in the group was wrestling with personally. Natalie didn't build a bridge, but she exposed the family's spiritual dysfunction in one sweeping statement, in a way that alienated her from the other family members.

By dropping this grenade in the group setting, Natalie blew away any foundation she might have started building for a bridge to crucial conversations. Mom had established the family's spiritual culture and she continued the family tradition of cultural Christianity. Every family member learned to "play Christian" at a young age, but now they were adults living as practical atheists. They were all living in ways similar to Dustin. The destructive results of this failed conversation were not only detrimental to the family, but also to Justin and Natalie's mission. This painful experience cast the young couple as yet another casualty of the Christian Army who attempt to share their faith, get rejected, and decide it's better to just keep their faith to themselves. Internally Natalie felt, "I am never going to try that again; that was too painful. I don't want to lose my family."

"Spiritual conversations should be our ultimate motive not our ulterior motive"

Natalie and Justin wanted to share their story with their family, but they never got that far. They looked for a chance, but were unprepared to share if the opportunity ever arose. No one had helped them, or coached them to develop their story well. In fact, theirs was a story of an amazing and personal transformation. It had not been refined enough to be laid bare before a spiritually hardened family. Their journey was filled with what I call awkward attempts to build a bridge.

AWKWARD ATTEMPTS TO BUILD A BRIDGE

Natalie and Justin had recently given their lives to Christ after a season of turmoil. During this season, they experienced a series of events that came together to give them confidence that they could trust Jesus with their lives, and their future. The weave of frenetic personal stories told them they could trust in the reality of a caring, loving God.

If they had built a bridge to their family, they did not have the skill to share in a sentence how their lives had been transformed. They could have said, "through a season of testing and difficulty God progressively revealed Himself to us, so that we were persuaded to trust Christ with our whole lives." They previously had tried to share their story by giving tedious details of every instance. When they boldly shared their tedious story they waited with big eyes and bated breath for an affirming response. They had hoped their series of awkward attempts to build a bridge would combine to persuade others that they too could trust Christ with their own lives. Like most Christians, Natalie and Justin just don't know how to tell their story.

One of the most painful experiences in church life is open mic night. As a kid I remember painful

> "People probably aren't saying no to Jesus as much as we think they are." Doug Pollock

times when an unprepared pastor would fill a service with "testimonies" from the congregation. Even as a young boy I remember thinking, "no Christians I know have any idea how to tell their story."

Try it sometime. Ask a Christ follower, "Tell me your story. How has Christ transformed your life?" Most people have no idea how to share such a basic, vital story. In our post-Christian culture if we don't learn how to tell our story, we are hosed. One of the most common ways that we send our stories into a confusing tailspin is what I call the "bizarre spiritual story."

We all have made awkward attempts to build a bridge. In doing so we have shared a convoluted series of seemingly unrelated events. The crazy string of occurrences are personal to us. They are things the Father used to convince you He can be trusted. They always seem to come out of right field. You don't see them coming, but somehow God uses them to point you to Himself. These events are personal and powerful.

The problem is they often don't translate well into our fuller story, especially if our audience is spiritually hardened. Our bizarre stories often give us some revelation and include a mystical element that very well may be divine intervention. We all have them. These events help us as Christ followers learn to place our full trust in the Father as He reveals Himself in a specific way that is personal to us.

The problem is that these stories are so personal they should never take the lead in a spiritual conversation. We've all heard well-meaning Christians tell some run on story that had us shaking our heads as we walked away. Some are whoppers. If I was a pagan, far from Christ with some measure of spiritual openness, after most Christians' awkward attempt to share their bizarre story, I think I'd double down on paganism.

 EXAMPLE #1 Awkward Attempts   I was in a church lobby when a 35-year-old new Christian cornered me to share his latest epiphany. He was making deliveries in his

work truck when he kept getting a sense that he needed to pull over and check his truck. He pulled into a rest stop and looked around his truck. He saw nothing out of the ordinary, so he got back in the cab and drove on. The same haunting sense kept stirring him. He decided to stop and check it out again. As he got out of the truck the second time the lugs on the front wheel snapped and the truck collapsed to the ground on the passenger side. Several of the lugs had stress fractures and in that moment the wheel failed.

This was an amazing story to hear! But I hope this young man didn't walk into work the next day leading with "God spoke to me and saved my life by wrecking my truck on the shoulder of the road instead of in traffic." A person who has never experienced promptings of the Holy Spirit might hear that story and think he simply had lost his mind.

EXAMPLE #2
Awkward Attempts

Angie, a striking, 38-year-old new Christian, had a similar story. She was an executive in a Fortune 500 company with a powerful story of how Christ had changed her life. People were drawn to her and the change that was happening in her. She loved to tell the story of how Christ was revealed to her as she drove down the road and saw a rainbow and weird cloud formations. Those revelations led her to move to that town beneath the rainbow where she met people from our new church plant. Through those relationships she surrendered her life to Christ and the Spirit of God dramatically changed her life.

This bizarre spiritual story was significant and intensely personal to her, and she was moved that the God of the universe was interested in the details of her life. She repeatedly told the story and repeatedly was disappointed that listeners were not nearly as moved as she was.

BRAIN TWEAK
Craft Your Story

With some coaching she re-crafted her story to be a powerful part of her crucial conversation toolbox. All she had to do was remove the unnecessary bizarre spiritual details and the story worked well. She learned to tell the story in a much more convincing way. With some work it went like this:

> *"There was a time in my life when I needed direction and guidance. I begged God to reveal Himself to me. Almost as I called out to the Father, He responded. He gave me some very personal affirmations and promptings. I decided to take a risk and I followed each prompting. With each faith step my confidence in the Father grew stronger. Those series of steps led me to an encounter with Jesus that changed my life. I also found a group of people who have walked with me in a way that has made all the difference."*

The second version of the story doesn't focus on the bizarre spiritual connection between her decision and the rainbow and clouds. Those personal elements were important to her because they prompted her to take a faith step. But it is much easier to identify with her story

when she mentions elements common to many – her
need for direction in a difficult time, allowing herself to
be led in a way that provided a new level of confidence in
the Father. This shift allowed the Holy Sprit to give her a
new perspective and enable her to make a significant
change in her life.

Before, she had let the rainbow and clouds become
a bizarre distraction to an otherwise great story. We must
learn how to tell our story in a way that lets others hear
what we really want to say.

 **EXAMPLE OF**
Bizarre Stories
My first bizarre spiritual story
occurred during my first year as a Christ
follower. My wife and I were praying about moving to
Israel as missionaries. We had tapped all of our resources
for the move and we still came up short. Our time to raise
the funds was up, so it looked like the move was off.

We just didn't have the money. We decided to pray
for the exact amount of money that we needed. We had
never prayed this specifically before, but soon after we
prayed, a person we had never met gave us the exact
amount due. He said as he prayed with a group of people,
our name came up and they were prompted to give us
this precise sum.

As far as I know they could not have known how
much we needed. That experience demonstrated that we
could trust the Father with the intimate details of our
lives.

I exuberantly told a version of that story with all the
details soon after it happened. There were many more

tedious details to the story and if I had a listener, I didn't leave any of them out.

This story was personal to me so the details seemed necessary to communicate the power of God. But when I told the story, very few found it as powerful as I did, because it was personal to me, not to them.

BRAIN TWEAK
Details Are Boring

One of the guys I was discipling broke the news to me one day. "I don't know if you are aware of it," he said. "But you bore people with all your God stories.

I had no idea what he was talking about. He helped me see that what I thought was an inspirational story that would help him grow in faith in Christ actually was detail overkill.

He worked with me to retell my story in a way that a guy like him would want to hear. He suggested that I tell it this way:

> *"As a young Christ follower my wife and I needed to learn to trust the Father for the details of our lives. We decided to trust the Father instead of our own human capacities to provide for us something we had been unable to provide for ourselves. Not long after we prayed, someone we had never met said that as he was praying, the Father told him to offer a gift to us that he had no way of knowing was the exact amount we needed. That event showed me that the Father is interested in the details of my life."*

The guy I was discipling helped me see that the streamlined second version of my story is a far better version because even a spiritually hardened person could connect with it. He helped me see it doesn't matter how amazing the story is if nobody is listening.

Ask yourself, "Do I really need to tell the full version of my story to perfect strangers?" My bizarre spiritual story is never the first card I lay down when someone genuinely wants to know why I am a Christ follower.

Can you imagine this exchange? "So, Dan, why are you so passionate about following Christ and going God's way in your life?"

> *"Well a stranger we had never met before named Fred handed us a check from God for $447, so we could move to Israel to become missionaries. That day God gave us the amount of money we needed, down to the penny. God manages my bank account now."*

That would sound strange to most people, especially for those who are far from Christ. Let's face it, most faith stories are a little bizarre to begin with. Too many people walk away shaking their head at the crazy, confused ramblings of most ill-prepared, but well intentioned Christians.

Crucial Questions

At the end of each chapter will be a few questions to prompt you to create your own crucial questions. These questions are prompts to build your skills to ask crucial questions and are not intended for you to memorize. I pray you continue to develop the skill of asking effective questions.

CRUCIAL QUESTIONS

CRUCIAL QUESTIONS
For Bridge Building

CRUCIAL QUESTIONS
OTHER BELIEF SYSTEMS

• What kind of belief system did your family have when you were growing up?

• Have you ever wondered how all religions can be equally right when they believe such different ideas?

• Have you ever wondered why there are so many different religions?

• Do you think it's possible for anyone to really know if there is a God?

CRUCIAL QUESTIONS
ABOUT DEATH

• It's been said that life is largely out of control. If that's true why do so many people try to control the uncontrollable?

• How do you want to be remembered at your funeral?

• If you could choose the manner of your death, how would you like to go?

• Does the thought of death scare you? [1]

---

[1] The Crucial Questions are adapted from Irresistible Evangelism Steve Sojourn, Dave Ping, Doug Pollock. 2001

"As they were leaving the synagogue, the people invited them to speak further about these things on the next Sabbath."
-Acts 13:42

"The church exists to engage a lost world in a conversation of redemption and hope."
-C.S. Lewis

CHAPTER 2

THE PRINCIPLE OF THE 42'S

I have begun to notice in the Bible how frequently the early Christ followers engaged in effective spiritual conversations. Most of them simply told their story. In most cases they make it brief and to the point.

EXAMPLE
Life Change
        I also noticed an odd pattern. It seems that almost every time a spiritual conversation is recorded in any chapter of Acts it happens in verse 42. This was a strange coincidence. I call this "the principle of the 42s."

I underlined the conversation words in the selected verse 42 passages in Acts where this principle occurs. In Acts 5:42 it says,

"Day after day…they never stopped <u>speaking about</u> and <u>sharing</u> the amazing news about Jesus…."

Armed with nothing more than their account of how Jesus changed their lives, they couldn't keep from talking about it. Acts 9:42 says,

"They <u>spoke</u> of what God had done all over Joppa, and many people believed in the Lord. "

These disciples simply helped others connect the dots of what the Father was up to. The new followers emphatically <u>proclaimed</u> in Acts 10:42,

"The Father compelled us to <u>speak</u> about these things to the people and to share our story, that Jesus is the one whom God appointed as judge of the living and the dead."

Even as they engaged the religious elite they found favor. In Acts 13:42

"As they were leaving the synagogue, the leaders invited them to <u>speak</u> further about the things God was up to the next time they gathered."

This group knew how to share in a relevant way. They simply spoke about their experience. The culture was hostile to them, yet they shared their story with respect and love.

These verses show us how early Christ followers built a bridge to those who were across the spiritual divide. They spoke and shared bravely about the one who had changed them. They explained how Jesus refocused a group of common fishermen to live a Kingdom-centered life. Spiritual conversations must center on the story of Jesus as told through your experience with Him.

Notice how many times it said in the book of Acts that the early church spoke and shared boldly. In Acts 2:42, it says the new followers were engaging in spiritual conversations and, they devoted themselves to the "apostles' teaching." Their devotion to the "apostles teaching" took the form of crucial conversations.

"It's seems we have forgotten that the early church existed for those who were yet to become Christ followers"

These early disciples simply related their personal stories. They had no Bibles. Most everything they knew about the Kingdom of God came from spiritual conversations as told to them by those who had been with Jesus. They shared their story with anyone who would listen.

They had no influence, social or academic credentials. All they had was their life change stories and the spiritual conversations that came as the Holy Spirit led them.

In short, learning to tell your story is your most valuable tool for making disciples. It becomes the first step in developing effective spiritual conversations. Life change stories were the primary tool of the early church and you should consider your life change story your primary tool as well.

THREE PARTS TO LIFE CHANGE STORIES

PAUL'S STORY
Three Parts

Consider the Apostle Paul's life change story. In the powerful style of *before I met Jesus, when I met Jesus, and after I met Jesus,* This is an example of how his story would go.

BEFORE HE MET JESUS

"I was ambitiously climbing the career ladder of Pharisaism, when I lost my way. I wrapped myself in the shroud of blind spiritual fanaticism. This led to the harsh behaviors of arrogant piety, condemnation, and judgementalism. I deceived myself to think that I had become the standard God wanted and approved. I had come to believe that if I destroyed the sect who followed Jesus called the people of 'the Way,' that I would be doing the greatest service to God."

WHEN HE MET JESUS

"All that changed when I met Jesus Christ in a flash that blinded me on a road to Damascus. He explained to me that I was persecuting the one I claimed to serve."

Notice that Paul doesn't elaborate on the sensational event of being struck down and blinded by a heavenly light. Nor does he hype the voice he heard of the resurrected Jesus. He describes this story three times in the book of Acts. He tells it in a simple way.

AFTER HE MET JESUS

Paul might have described his transformation by saying, "Since that time I have come to realize how powerful is this thing called grace. I went from a self-righteous persecutor to a fully convinced recipient of amazing grace. I can never be the same again."

You may say that now we read and study the Bible instead of having spiritual conversations. Both cases can transfer information, but the two methods are very different. Relationships develop around conversation. And, the foundation for discipleship is relationship, not information transfer. The primary tool early followers had for creating life change were crucial conversations.

LEARN TO TELL YOUR STORY/TESTIMONY

 EXAMPLE
Tell Your Story: As I pulled up to the Tex-Mex cantina, just off the beach near my house, I said out loud, "Father I've been coming here for several weeks to see if I could develop any crucial conversations with the staff. If you want me to move on to another restaurant I will. Just know that I'm completely available."

That day I met Kat, she was the manager of the establishment. She was warm and open. She was a California girl and a Mormon. We quickly struck up a conversation about being from California. In our first conversation I began to ask her several questions about mormonism. That opened up the door for me to share my story. I scheduled many of my appointments at the cantina. This gave me a chance to keep the conversation going with Kat who worked every day at lunch. Over the next few weeks I got to know her story. She had two daughters and had been living with a local doctor for some time. She quickly moved from polite to interested when it came to spiritual matters. Before long she said, "Ok, how does this thing work?" I shared a deeper level of my story with her and began to talk about the life change that can happen when you step across the threshold of faith to trust Christ. I think we talked for an hour that day.

The Holy Spirit was at work in Kat in a major way. Before long she was engaging her boyfriend in life change conversation. They decided after a prolonged time of living together that they should marry. I never mentioned the subject to her. The wedding plans opened up some great chances to talk openly about the changes that were occurring in their lives.

Over the next couple of months of discipling conversations the boyfriend came to Christ as well. Six months later they were married and baptized.

From the start she mastered the art of telling her story simply, like the blind man who was healed by Jesus. "Once I was a Mormon living under the pressure of legalism and condemnation," she would say. "I met Jesus and He has set me free."

She freely shared her story with anyone who seemed open. Kat was a people magnet, drawing others to her like a monkey to a cup cake. Before long she and her husband were helping to plant a church. This newly married couple had experienced an amazing change in their lives from a simple encounter at a local Mexican grill and now were among the founding core of a church plant.

THE FRIENDSHIP FACTOR

CONVERSATIONS
Where We-Live Work-Play

Why is it so easy for Kat to initiate spiritual conversations? She simply looked for crucial conversations where she lived, worked and played. She put energy into befriending others. It might look easy for her to make friends; but, she is intentional about cultivating relationships.

Everyone can make friends. It's as simple as what you learned to do in pre-school when you just walked up to another kid and began to connect. "Whatcha doin?" "Can I play?" It really is that simple.

Somewhere along the way – probably about the time of puberty – you likely lost the innocent brashness to simply connect with others. That's a time when we become painfully self-aware and feel socially awkward. When you were five you weren't socially awkward, you were just social.

About the time you started feeling self-conscious you decided the job of connecting with others about Jesus was reserved for spiritual superstars who can muscle a faith discussion into any conversation. If you are like most of us you've told yourself, "I don't do well when I am put on the spot. I don't know what to say. I need to learn more about the Bible. I am spiritually awkward. I don't have what it takes."

Every day we pass countless familiar faces without stopping to learn their names or hear their stories. We see this sea of faces at the gym, at work, in the local grocery, and in restaurants. What might happen if you decided simply to pause long enough to say a word, to seed a connection with them, to build a bridge across the divide? What could happen if I made it my goal to get to know them and discover how many secretly long to know the Father and to become growing disciples.

Getting started

You might ask an opening question that discerns a person's spiritual receptivity. In the past, church members have been encouraged to "share the gospel" to reach people who are far from Christ. This sounds like it should work, and in theory, you're right. But if you interviewed all the pastors in America they would tell you 98 percent of their people never have spiritual conversations. The ones that do, harvest little or no fruit from their efforts.

A good, hard comparison between the New Testament church and modern churches reveals one startling difference. The New Testament church grew explosively largely with one tool – followers shared their personal life change story. The "principle of the 42's" was virtually all they had to reach a hostile world that wanted to hunt, identify and execute them.

First century converts didn't have attractive church services to which they could invite friends. They had no Christian radio stations, or arena concert events. They had no access to much of the scriptures. Their cell leaders were not educated. They had virtually no financial resources.

Our well-resourced churches do not come close to producing the results that these first century Christians produced. The strategic difference is that the New Testament church invested its energy cultivating the life change stories of those who had encountered Jesus. They dispersed into the world and sought crucial conversations with people, telling them the good news of their life change.

Our primary problem is that most pastors can only identify a hand full of members who have been radically changed by the Spirit of God. If Christians do not have a life transformation story they will not be able to have crucial conversations.

In the absence of such a story, church members will talk about church and religious events. Their well meaning conversations will not draw those far from Christ. Often those conversations will include a tone of judgment, condemnation, and an occasional sermonette.

Your most essential element for effective spiritual conversation is evidence of Christ's transforming work in your life. There is no substitute for the work of the Spirit in the life of a follower. No training can take the place of what happens when our life is genuinely changed.

There will be no reproduction, or effective spiritual movement in the life of a person who has not been changed by the work of the Holy Spirit. Please stop and prayerfully consider two questions on which this entire process hinges.

First: Do I have a life change story because I am a submitted disciple, who has been changed by the indwelling Holy Spirit?

Second: Am I convinced the people I will encounter today need and desire to engage in spiritual conversations?

If you can't answer yes to those two questions I encourage you to lay down this book and allow the Spirit of God to begin a fresh work in you starting now.

Perhaps you can point to a time in the past where the work of the Spirit was fresh and alive in you. Too often Christ followers once aflame get distracted, weighed down, consumed with life's details and they lose focus. I call this the condition of the shrinking heart.

Fatigue, sin and unbelief can cause a shrinking heart. Nothing else in this book will help if you have launched a secret rebellion in your heart. Allow the Spirit to breathe new life into you, and surrender so He can create your soul to hunger after Christ.

EVERY CONVERSATION CAN BE A SPIRITUAL CONVERSATION

I have met with church planters who tell me the people living where they are trying to launch a work won't participate in spiritual conversations. They're too spiritually hardened.

People have spiritual conversations all the time. Our own lack of awareness is the primary culprit, not the absence of people willing to engage in spiritual conversations.

Once you develop the skill of listening, you will find people have been holding spiritual conversations all around you but you weren't tuned in to recognize them. You will discover you're drowning in opportunities.

Sure, some places are spiritually tougher than others. But it's a universal truth that people long to know how they are here and why. You have that for a starting place with anyone!

Ecclesiastes 3:11 tells us that all people were made for spiritual conversations. It reminds us that the Holy Spirit of God, "has set eternity in the human heart." That means, every one of us has a drive to know and discuss the eternal aspect of our lives.

THE THREE RELATIONSHIP STEPS

BRAIN TWEAK
Relate Naturally

Without trying to codify something that can occur naturally, let me say that making such connections is a three-step process:

- Make the effort to introduce yourself

- Show interest in hearing their story

- Explore whether they can be discipled

Each of us has friends and acquaintances who are living far from the Father. They face an eternity without Christ. Christ followers long for their friends to know the life changing love of Jesus, they just don't know how to take the next step to lead them there. In fact few are making any progress in this most critical area. That's not because they don't see the need to point people toward the Father, they just struggle with how to get it done.

There seems to be a cycle in Christian life that the longer a person is involved in a church, the fewer spiritual conversations they hold. There is something wrong with this trend. It should track the opposite way. Bill Hybels, founder and senior pastor of Willow Creek Community Church, created this graph to illustrate the trend. The horizontal axis represents in years how long you have walked with Christ. The vertical axis represents the amount of quality contacts you have with people who are living far from God.[2]

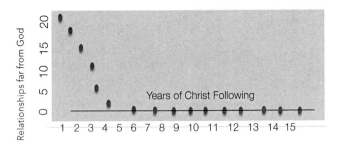

After just a few years as a Christian, the number of connections we have with non-Christians drops to virtually zero. The pace of our lives and the comfort of our Christian circle seems to edge out any urgency to engage in meaningful conversations.

Most Christians confess they feel unqualified or ill-equipped for one of Jesus' essential instructions. He said, *"As you go make disciples." Matt 28:19*

²Hybels, Bill, Just Walk Across the Room: Simple Steps Pointing People to Faith (Grand Rapids:Zondervan) 2006 p.61

We all feel the separation in the divide that happens between us and those who are far from Christ. You probably agree that disciple making should be a distinguishing mark of a Christ-follower. But what if you feel inadequate to accomplish this command? You and I were created to make disciples. We just have to unlearn some negative we've learned. Some believe mistakenly that only Bible scholars who can recall chapter and verse on command can hold spiritual conversations.

Look at the spiritual conversations recorded in the New Testament, uneducated peasants simply telling their story with easy dialogue. If Jesus had believed the key ingredient for disciple making was Bible information, He would have invited the Pharisees and Sadducees to be His disciples. As it turns out Jesus didn't invite any of those folks into His first community. He clearly doesn't think Bible knowledge alone makes you a disciple. Disciples are followers who are filled with the Spirit of God and are willing to grow in obedience. This type of person will read and absorb the scriptures but putting scripture knowledge first gets this backwards. We don't have to know much scripture to begin the adventure of obeying Jesus. When we share our faith we will become effective disciples.

Are you trying to cut a deal with God to get off the spiritual conversation hook? Some say, "God, I will read the Bible and become a biblical encyclopedia if that's what it takes. I'll help the poor. I will go on a mission trip every summer. In fact, I'll volunteer at church every week if you will let me off the spiritual conversation/ discipleship hook."

I feel so sad just writing about this trend. We don't realize that we can't grow in our relationship with the Father if we avoid the process of spiritual conversations that will lead us to make disciples. These two elements create growth and maturity in a Christ follower. When we get connected to the reproduction of other Christ followers we become vibrant, alive disciples.

MY MOST SELFISH DAY

I reached the pinnacle of selfishness the day I got married. You could say it was my most selfish day. I'll bet it was yours as well. I thought that I was a mature adult when I was single. I had life figured out. I thought I was a kind, loving adult. The day I got married was the last day I could make everything be about me. As a single guy, I did what I wanted to do. I went where I wanted to go. I spent my money the way I wanted. I bought a sports car. Everything was about me. That all changed on my wedding day. Now I had to include someone else in my decisions. Before long there were two little mini-me's running around.

The cool car was gone and a mini van was parked in its spot. With kids in tow, every decision went through the matrix of how it affected the family.

It is amazing how "other people" focused I became. I felt responsible for these little lives I helped bring into the world. In a spiritual sense, when we engage in crucial conversations and making disciples we can't help but grow.

REPRODUCTION BREAKS SELFISHNESS

BRAIN TWEAK
We Mature When
We Reproduce

When we shift our focus from ourselves toward investing in someone else we can't help but change. The same is true spiritually. When we engage in the initial step of reproduction, which is a crucial conversation with a person far from Christ, we begin the reproduction process. The self-centered, classic cultural Christianity lifestyle never produces real spiritual maturity. The Father has designed the process of spiritual reproduction to grow and develop us. When we reproduce we develop a bonding concern for the wellbeing of someone other than ourselves. That will always create maturity in us.

I have met Christians who think they are mature because they have biblical knowledge and can articulately discuss theology and doctrine. We only really grow when we engage in spiritual reproduction and discipleship.

Scores of church attenders convince themselves they are mature Christians. Yet they bear little to no sense of responsibility about reaching people who face a Christ-less eternity.

I am amazed at the number of Christians who not only avoid talking with people who have different lifestyles, but a shocking number actually get annoyed with people who don't know Christ. A person in that condition, of course will embrace values and behaviors of which a Christ follower does not approve. Are you one who resists walking toward people who need God's transformational love because you're offended by their social causes, lifestyle, or political views? Jesus ran toward these people. He had every intention of building a bridge to them. I am shocked at how many who call themselves Jesus followers have an aversion to nonbelievers. It seems the divide that separates them from those far from Christ is not on their radar. It is not right to hide in foxholes to avoid the very people Jesus came to redeem. Building bridges to span the divide means that I must learn to think differently. I must be the disciple before I can make disciples like Jesus said to do.

I MUST FIRST BE THE DISCIPLE

If we're going to engage in crucial conversations with others it has to start inside *us*. We must become safe people to create the kind of openness that produces effective conversations. Romans 12:2 says that when we become available to the work of Christ in us we will be, "transformed by the renewing of our minds." The result of this work will be that we will know and follow the Father's will and heart. Jesus demonstrated that the Father sent Him and likewise He sent us to seek those who have become separated from the Father (Luke 19:10). If we're going to have crucial conversations they must begin in us.

Unfortunately, we're cautious and afraid to surrender our list of entitlements. We struggle to think differently about our friendships and our relatives. We protest, it's *my* money, *my* time, *my* needs. We won't engage in life giving crucial conversations until we've allowed the Father to do a crucial work in us first.

BRAIN TWEAK
I Must Be The Disciple

When I become a disciple, my thought process changes. I am no longer trying to do something to someone else. I am obediently responding to the commission Jesus gave me. He said, "As you go make disciples." When I stop worrying about trying to share my faith and just respond as a disciple who loves to tell the story of how Christ changed his life, I will find people respond differently. With that approach I become a safe person who is just sharing my story. People trust a safe person. The Father uses safe people to create safe conversations.

When we try to force faith, doctrine, or beliefs on people we stop being a disciple and become spiritual timeshare salesmen. We will run over the person with whom we are talking. Culture already views Christians as a people who push their beliefs on others, according to Barna research. They said, "Like it or not, being unyielding and judgmental is intricately connected to our image as Christians…an entire generation of those inside and outside the church are questioning our motives… They say Christians are more focused on condemning people than helping people become more like Jesus. We have lost something in the way we communicate."

Based on a survey, a majority of outsiders (57 percent) say Christians are quick to find fault with others.[3] Being judgmental pushes people away from God's purposes, and people become repulsed by an image of Jesus that is not at all like the real thing. "When Christians are judgmental, arrogant and quick to find fault, we are unChristian."

INTRODUCING THE ICON CULTURE

ICON TOOL BOX
A New Way To Communicate

The tool box represents a practical idea or icon that you can use in your conversations in a post literate culture.

People used to read lots of books and magazines. That's no longer true, but it doesn't mean we have less information. We're just not as good at discerning what's important through the constant inundation of trivia.

My college friend Mark Snowden has researched the American post-literate culture. In his popular book, *"Truth that Sticks"* he says, "We are all aware that people are increasingly choosing to receive information in non-print forms. Because we are reading less we are reading with much less comprehension. Even though the majority of Americans can read, many are becoming less literate.[4]

The U.S. Department of Education researched 18,500 people and determined that fewer than half of all Americans can handle "continuous prose"—and it is estimated that the Bible is 75 percent continuous prose... Learning to communicate significant concepts through

3 Kinnaman, David; Lyons, Gabe. UnChristian: What a New Generation Really Thinks about Christianity...and Why It Matters (Kindle Locations 2961-2962). Baker Publishing Group. 2007 Kindle Edition.

4 Avery Willis;Mark Snowden. Truth That Sticks: How to Communicate Velcro Truth in a Teflon World (LifeChange) (Kindle Locations 111-116). Kindle Edition.

non-literary means will be critical in sharing Biblical truths and principles.

Researchers say 20 million people have completely stopped reading "continuous prose". That means that, at this rate, we are losing the capacity to communicate with a million people a year through traditional literary methods. The largest drop in reading rates is among young adults, ages 18-24."[5]

Most people in Jesus' time were pre-literate, where a huge number in our time are post-literate. Most in our culture know how to read. The trend of social media and the wider Internet has prompted us to read differently than our parents. Now we often see words in combination with graphic images to illustrate the words. Without knowing it we have begun as a society to communicate differently.

The more things change the more we reflect the past. Jesus also combined words and images to communicate complex eternal truths about a new kingdom He was ushering in.

Using Icons in crucial conversations

ICON TOOL BOX
Building Skill

This section is called the icon toolbox. At the end of each section you will see an icon you can use in a crucial conversation. This tool will assist you in communicating your story along with a biblical truth.

---

[5]Ibid

THE ICON TOOL BOX

Each icon can be used to enhance your story. They usually are what I call "napkin art." That is, they work best in a casual setting. Let's say you are sharing a meal and a crucial conversation breaks out. You can grab a napkin and draw an icon to illustrate a biblical truth in a way that cuts through verbiage and creates spiritual movement.

You can learn, remember and repeat icons. Jesus referred to and used common elements from our sensory world. He taught deep spiritual truths through parables with common items, such as seeds, soil, and weeds.

Icons helped leaders of the pre-literate Church to build a biblical worldview among followers. Early icons were crude symbols and images but they communicated biblical truth. As the process matured, artists were commissioned to paint biblical scenes as great works of art. But early Christ followers used simple symbols to communicate basic truths of scripture, most notably the cross and fish.

YOUR BRAIN

Your brain is a mysterious thing. It's almost as if the Father created a velcro learning system for us. Velcro was invented by George de Mestral in Switzerland. During a vacation in 1944, he took his dog for a walk. When he returned, he had to pull cockleburs from his dog's fur. De Mestral took one of the burs and put it under a microscope. He noticed that tiny hooks covered the bur's surface; when these hooks hit the loops of his dogs fur, they stuck tightly. It took 10 years to figure out how to manufacture the system of tiny nylon hooks and loops that he called Velcro. If you look at a piece of Velcro, you will see that one side has loops and the other has hooks.

Our brains are equipped with high learning capacity – call it hooks if you will. Jesus communicated in a way that produced contagious learning – call it loops. When you put them together you get the velcro of the gospel.

BRAIN TWEAK
Velcro Learning

At age one, Cambria began to speak a phrase we had never heard. Our family began to play a game with her. We stacked eight blocks and she would knock them over and shout a phrase we could not understand. She repeated it every time she knocked over the block tower. It sounded like French, but no one in the family spoke French.

Three weeks later my oldest daughter noticed that the language on video she played while Cambria slept had been accidentally switched from English to French. All night long while she slept she was learning French. She found a way to include the phrase into her vocabulary in perfect context. Her words formed a celebration phrase the equivalent of "oh joy." Her little brain of hooks had latched onto the loops of words until they worked their way into her vocabulary.

If this is how the Father built our brains to work we should build a system of learning that works in sync with how we were made to learn. Jesus mastered this style of learning. He presented ideas in loop fashion so our brain hooks could embrace and retain His critical content. He knew we would not easily grasp complex spiritual truths that would seem like foreign words to us. So He wrapped them in ideas and stories that were visual, and tangible.

In each chapter we will provide you an accompanying image you can learn to draw. You can use these images to tell your story.

The Bridge Icon

ICON TOOL BOX
The bridge Icon

When I am in a crucial conversation and I sense that I can share my story, one of the first tools I recommend is the bridge icon. Remember, an icon is a straight forward, simple, visual tool to illustrate a story. By itself, no icon is going to take anyone through the steps a person must take to repent and receive the Holy Spirit. But they are helpful tools.

Here is how I might share my story using the bridge icon: "I was living my life apart from the Father. I knew deep inside that something kept separating me from being the person I wanted to be. I never knew why I always felt distant from the Father. Someone finally explained that there really is a great chasm between the Father and me. It wasn't my imagination. That divide was created by my drive to live life in a way that was really a form of rebellion against God's way.

"The Bible word is 'sin.' Sin is not about individual behaviors. It is much deeper than actions.

"I didn't like the gnawing sense of distance between me and the Father. I just didn't know how to leap over the chasm. I tried morality. It just left me feeling like a loser. I finally realized that no amount of effort on my part could get me to the other side. Someone suggested that I finally give up trying on my own, and allow Jesus to serve as the bridge. Jesus came to be our bridge to the Father. He came to close the gap we experience between us and a perfect God."

Fractured Life   God's Life

The most important thing to remember is to have a crucial conversation, not a theology lesson. Don't worry about backing it up with supporting verses. Just tell your story using the idea that you and the Father were separated by a chasm, you were aware of the gap, and you realized only Jesus could close it.

Anyone can use the bridge icon, because it is the heart and soul of the gospel message. Think about how you can share your story using the bridge icon. If your story is anything like mine, before you met Christ you probably felt a gnawing separation from the Father. If that is the case, you probably spent a chunk of time collecting building materials on your side of the chasm with no idea how to span the gulf. That did not deter me from planning to get to God with my own grand bridge building scheme.

We all have a story about our own bridge building plans. But we're transformed when we abandon the idea of using the inadequate bricks of a moral life and we simply walk across the bridge that Christ built for us. It comes to this one truth: your past does not disqualify you. Your future can be different by simply abandoning your own construction project and trusting Christ's. The Father says your moral bricks are inadequate. "All our righteous acts are like filthy rags." Isaiah 64:6. Simply pick up your lunch bucket, toss your hard hat, leave your work site and walk across a bridge that has been so lovingly provided for you.

CRUCIAL QUESTIONS

CRUCIAL QUESTIONS
For Bridge Building

CRUCIAL QUESTIONS ABOUT GOD

• Have you ever noticed that what most people believe about God is not in the Bible?

• Why do you think there are so many misconceptions about God?

• Do you think that we can be loved by God unconditionally?

• Has your belief or disbelief in God affected your life?

CRUCIAL QUESTIONS HOW TO FOLLOW JESUS

• Based on your understanding, how does someone become a Christian and follow Jesus?

• Have you ever thought about what it means to be a Christian or to follow Jesus?

• Have you ever explored what the Bible has to say about how someone follows Jesus and becomes a Christian?

CRUCIAL

crucial

conversations

CHANGING

HOW WE TELL
OUR STORY

SECTION 2

STORY OF MAN BORN BLIND
JOHN 9:7-36

John 9:7 Jesus placed mud on the blind mans eyes and sent him to the Temple pool to wash. "…His neighbors and those who had formerly seen him begging asked, "Isn't this the same man who used to sit and beg?"…he himself insisted, "I am the man." "How then were your eyes opened?" they asked. He replied, "The man they call Jesus made some mud and put it on my eyes. He told me to go to Siloam and wash. So I went and washed, and then I could see.

John 9:25-27 One thing I do know. I was blind but now I see!" Then they asked him, "What did he do to you? How did he open your eyes?" He answered, "I have told you already and you did not listen. Why do you want to hear it again? Do you want to become his disciples too?

John 9:30 Now that is remarkable! You don't know where he comes from, yet he opened my eyes.

John 9:35-38 Jesus heard that they had thrown him out, and when he found him, he said, "Do you believe in the Son of Man?" "Who is he, sir?" the man asked. "Tell me so that I may believe in him. Jesus said, "You have now seen him; in fact, he is the one speaking with you."Then the man said, "Lord, I believe," and he worshiped him.

"You can do more with 12 transformed disciples than with 1,200 religious consumers"
-Alan Hirsch

"When I tell my story does it have the tendency to cause people to want to follow Jesus?"
-Dallas Willard

CHAPTER 3

CRUCIAL CONVERSATIONS ABOUT A LIFE CHANGE STORY

CONVERSATIONS
The Man Born Blind

The scorching heat of the midday sun baked down on the group that followed Jesus as they moved through the throngs of visitors. The city hummed and vibrated as eager shoppers moved through the market. Shouts of vendors pierced the deafening noise of the crush, trying to attract buyers who moved systematically shop to shop.

The gaggle clinging to Jesus turned the corner and nearly stumbled over a blind beggar sitting in their path. They paused and began to discuss the cause of his deformity without thinking or caring that he could hear them.

Jesus explained that their worldview had gone off the rails. The man's blindness was neither punishment for the failures of his parents, nor recompense for his personal sin. This was instead an opportunity for the "Father to be at work." Jesus reminded them that every conversation is an opportunity for the Father, "to be at work."

To demonstrate his point, Jesus spat on the ground, made some mud with the saliva, and put it on the blind man's eyes. "Go," Jesus told him. "Wash in the Pool of Siloam." The man did as Jesus said, and miraculously, he came home seeing.

Let's join the disciples as we watch the aftermath of this event. The man immediately begins to share his story. Isn't that the most natural thing in the world? To share with others the miraculous restoration of his sight? He did not shrink back from telling his story, nor did he embellish it. He simply said, "I was blind and now I can see."

Those around him investigated his story to absurd lengths. Incredulous religious leaders kept asking the man in different ways how he came to see. He simply tells people about Jesus. Interestingly, a life change story doesn't have to be dramatic. It just has to be short, coherent and about the change Jesus made.

Religious leaders will not accept the man's story at face value. They dissect it to the point of his exasperation. He finally says as plainly as he knows how, "One thing I do know, I was blind but now I see!" They still do not accept it. The man asserts,

> *"I have told you already and you did not listen. Why do you want to hear it again? Do you want to become his disciples too?"…"It is remarkable! You don't know where he comes from, yet he opened my eyes."*
>
> John 9:27, 30.

He is virtually saying, "You guys act like you've got exclusive rights on God. It seems to scare you that you can't control this new prophet Jesus." Then they asked him,

> *"What did he do to you? How did he open your eyes?"*

They are acting like lawyers looking for a loophole to ensnare Jesus, and disqualify the man's story. They attack his credibility, claiming he was

> *"steeped in sin at birth; how dare you lecture us! And they threw him out."*   -John 9:31

BRAIN TWEAK
Share Your Story

Without any training the blind man clearly shared the elements of his life change story. He discovered the transforming power of the gospel at work in his life. Jesus invites him to embrace what had begun in him in a more full and complete way. Jesus invites him to trust in Him. "Then the man said, 'Lord, I believe,' and he worshiped Him." John 9:38.

The Father uses simple things to move us to surrender to His transforming power. The strength of this story is not just the healing. The man himself was changed. When we take the risk to tell our story something happens inside of us. The Spirit goes to work unraveling our old self and making way for the new.

In our story we must draw a critical contrast: What difference has Christ really made in your life? What were you like *before* Christ, and now what are you like *after* you've surrendered to Christ? The most vital change for the blind man happened after his spiritual eyes were opened.

EVERYONE LOVES A STORY

Peoples' stories fascinate us. All movies and TV shows are simply about a story that captivates you. Reality shows are nothing more than the unfolding of an unscripted story. We never out grow the fascination that comes from hearing a good story. Preschoolers chant to their weary parents, "Read it again, again." And we never outgrow that desire to hear a good story.

The heart of any quality entertainment medium is its ability to transmit a good story – whether via a movie, book, or song. Any form of entertainment not supported by a good story will soon fail.

I worked for a few years in radio and TV. It was easy to see that the most persuasive advertisements were always about a personal testimony. When a person looks into the camera's eye to tell you, "I was fluffy and now look at me. I lost 55 pounds vibrating on a piece of plastic in my living room instead of eating funnel cakes," it gets our attention. Every one of us is trying to discern how life works best. We want to learn a takeaway from a story that will help us in life. We all want to know "What made you decide to…?"

Most people live life making few, if any, changes year after year. When someone actually makes a change that lasts, it gets our attention. We all want to know how that shift made your life different. What is the catalyst dropped in between your before and your after? The best stories transport me into the heart of the issue.

LEARN TO TELL YOUR STORY SIMPLY

If your life has been changed natural opportunities will arise for you to share why you are so pumped about what Jesus is doing in your life. When that happens, tell it as simply as possible.

The three parts to your story are:
- What was going on before you met Christ?
- Why did you surrender your resistance against God?
- How has your life been since you began to follow Jesus?

Surprisingly, your story details don't have to be dramatic. Just keep it concise, on point, and relevant to the situation. How many times do you think the blind man told his story? I assure you he told that simple story, over and over again. In this passage alone he tells it four times in just one day.

BRAIN TWEAK
Craft Your Story

The blind guy mastered the art of the concise story. He doesn't get off track. He nails the story in twelve words. His obvious transformation makes him noticeable, his honesty makes him relatable, his brevity makes him interesting. He didn't know much about Jesus yet, but he said,

"One thing I do know. I was blind but now I see" -John 9:25.

That's all that was necessary to start the ripple of a movement. It was brief and personal. Each of us has the story of our experience with Christ.

Too many Christians make it harder than it needs to be. They shrink back from saying anything because they are afraid they don't know enough theology, or Bible. They fear being pushy or appearing stupid.

 **BRAIN TWEAK**
Your Story Can
Change Lives
 Remember, your story is powerful when you simply share what He has done in your life. That will be the most influential part of your spiritual conversation.

You'll uncover the most significant element of your story when you take time to contemplate where and when God began His work in you. This will be the first major step in your becoming a reproducing disciple.

When Jesus first changed my life I told everyone who would listen. But, even at that early stage I was afraid I would transform into a weird, spiritually irrelevant rambler. I was concerned that people would dismiss me like I had seen them dismiss so many who came off as Jesus weirdoes. It didn't matter. I had to share what happened to me. I had died twice in surgery and lived to tell about it. I went from being an invalid to full recovery. I knew that line alone, if not told correctly, would sound overly sensational. To make things worse, I had a story to tell about an experience I had while they were defibrillating me and trying to bring me back.

I was in surgery for facial reconstruction from an injury I received while being a practice dummy on the Georgetown College basketball team. While they were trying to remove my nose from my left eye socket where a flying elbow had deposited it, I coded on the surgical table. That's doctor speak for my heart stopping. That curious series of facts is like the blind guy's story. The background details don't matter. He didn't start by saying, "I showed up to beg like any other day. Then I heard a ruckus. Jesus stopped to answer a moral question that his disciples raised." He just got to the point. "I was blind and now I see." His statement implied, "That's the fact. Deal with that. How does your world explain it?"

The power of the blind man and of my story does not lie in tedious medical details. I usually don't go into my out-of-body experience during surgery. Instead, I use the relatable fact that I once was absolutely certain the only way to gain God's favor was to perform, achieve, and strive. The Father used an event that got my attention and sent me on a journey that changed my life.

The point of my story is not its sensational elements. The story has power because I met the Son of God in a way that changed me for here and eternity. Almost immediately it brought an overwhelming peace to my soul, an end to my useless striving, and a revolutionary change to my entire world.

I wanted to invest my life helping people discover the transformation that occurs when they surrender their life to the living person of Jesus Christ. That simple action made my life and story make sense. The missing piece for most us is we don't see how our story fits into God's greater story. When people grasp the big picture of how the work of the Father has direct implications for the meaning of their life stories, the light goes on.

I realized, wow, my life matters! Jesus didn't just come to lift the shackles off the shoulders of the desperate first century person. He can speak to my broken situation. I can receive "living water" that refreshes. It was a relief to realize Jesus is not looking for heroic displays of faith and obedience. He will engage us despite the fact we have nothing to offer Him. The good news I was given to share is that anyone can be restored, made whole, and welcomed home.

Build Your story

 TOOL BOX
Building My Story

Use the exercise on the next page to review and summarize your story by finishing the phrases: before I met Jesus, when I met Jesus, and how I've changes after I met Jesus. As you do this activity, remember it's important to make your spiritual journey relatable to someone who may not yet be a follower of Christ. Don't give unnecessary details. Share only elements that are broadly relatable. Don't share disconnected spiritual information or "weird" spiritual encounters.

THREE PARTS TO YOUR STORY

Finish each sentence:

Before I met Jesus...

When I met Jesus...

How I've changes since I met Jesus...

Crucial Questions

Crucial questions
Dealing with the un-explainable

• Have you ever seen a situation that was unexplainable?

• How did God fit into your view of what happened?

• What things raise your skepticism flag?

• As people get to know you what do they enjoy most about you?

Crucial questions
Getting to know you

• What do most people not know about you?

• What do most people not know about what you like to do?

• If you could change something about your past what would it be?

• Do you ever struggle with trying to control things?

• What kind of things do you think can be controlled in life?

"Day after day…they never stop speaking about, and
sharing the amazing news about Jesus."
-Acts 5:42

"What we need is not intellectual theorizing or even
preaching, but a real life story of how God can change actually a
life."
-Elton Trueblood

CHAPTER 4

BASIC MISTAKES TELLING OUR STORY

I often wonder what would happen if Christ followers would create low-risk, high-grace places for people to address their spiritual needs and to have crucial conversations. For some reason, we tend to invert that formula.

BRAIN TWEAK
Inverting The Formula

The Barna research group concluded a few years back that Christ followers are known for creating low grace, high judgment conversations. It's odd and too bad that we have become known for the opposite virtues for which Jesus was known. This has contributed to the relational divide that exists between Christians and the secular world. We have become known for things Jesus and the first century movement avoided.

In the book *UnChristian*, Kinnaman and Lyons say when outsiders think of Christians, "they think of our moralizing, our condemnations, and our attempts to draw boundaries around everything."[6] These behaviors are never associated with Jesus, by observers in the New Testament.

The existing Christian culture has contributed to a way of thinking and responding that has caused us to become more disconnected and less able to relate to those immersed in the current secular culture. A bridge must be built to close this relational divide.

There are seven mistakes we commonly make when we venture into the unfamiliar waters of spiritual conversations. When we talk to spiritually hardened people these mistakes shut down spiritual progress. Our low grace, high judgment language has become infused into the vocabulary of most Christians without their knowledge. Natalie and Justin are a perfect example of a conversation that appears to be low grace, high judgment. They have no idea they are embracing this new way of thinking. At the same time great things are developing in them. They are cultivating a solid Biblical world view. In the process of learning to think differently Natalie embraced some of the bad habits of those who went before her. Learning to translate our new world view into a language that reflects the mission of Jesus will take some effort. In the next chapter I'll suggest ways to tell your story that won't embarrass God and will help you build a bridge.

I celebrate that people want to share their stories. I rejoice in the God who gave them stories to tell. But when eternity is at stake for our listeners, I argue that we must do a better job of telling our stories. These are a few of the ways our stories miss the mark.

MISTAKE #1:
ABSENCE OF RELATABLE
POINTS OF CONTACT

BRAIN TWEAK
Building Skill

Most personal stories are boring, not because there is no genuine life change to share, but because the storyteller makes no effort to find a connection point with the listener. Where do you connect with your listener? Find a connection point to arouse their interest. To communicate effectively you should ask questions and listen to the responses. "Listening" doesn't mean waiting for a pause so you can jump in with your own observations. If you listen, you will hear their heart. The Apostle Paul knew his audiences. He found connection points from which he could share his experience. For a great example, see Acts 17:16-33.

We don't feign an interest in people so we can pressure them into a conversation about Christ. We want sincerely to know and understand people because they matter to the Father. The Father's love for them requires us to connect at whatever point they are willing to connect.

Finding relatable points of interest is what Jesus did when he connected with the woman at the well regarding the eternal refreshment that life giving water can provide.

I got to know a New York Times reporter as we flew cross county. As our conversation unfolded, he asked me why I seemed to love teaching pastors and leaders. I knew enough about him to guess accurately his objections to faith. I made an effort to share my story in a way that revealed I had wrestled with the claims of Christ personally and learned that I could follow Christ and still be intellectually sound.

He said, "You probably would never have guessed it, but I was raised in the church. My dad was a pastor and left us to marry the church secretary. I blindly accepted Christianity as a child, but as an adult I have blindly rejected faith." I told him I respected his honesty and said I had been changed by a community of Christ followers who were willing to live in an honest and open way.

He wiped away a tear and said, "If I could find that kind of a community I think I would consider exploring the claims of Christ. If they are as credible as you say, I could see myself coming back to Christ."

"It is more than great community," I told him. "I have a powerful friendship with the person of Jesus. I am not the same; I have been made new."

In that moment I no longer needed to relate or investigate. I was now free to briefly share the hope that is within me. He reflected and said, "You have given me some important things to think about." He quickly changed the topic to a more comfortable subject. We soon landed, as we were deplaning, he said, thank you for our conversation, I hope to find what you have found. I think I will start looking.

I asked him if I could give him my copy of "The God Questions" and he thanked me and said, I think I will read this. I had written my name and email address in the front cover of the book. I told him that my info was there, and I would love to hear from him. It wasn't long before He sent me an email back thanking me, and we have had some correspondence since.

That conversation opened up because a couple of relatable details were shared. Too many genuinely transformed Christ followers aren't aware of how powerful their story can be. They can't seem to identify the relatable details in their story. They need some help learning to tell their story. We will develop those skills later in the book.

Mistake #2:
An unfocused story

Most faith stories I hear are too long and too unfocused. People who give you a green light to share your story don't expect to be Social Security eligible when you finish.

Make your story brief. I know every detail matters to you, but frankly, minute details get in the way of the grand story. Your life change story should be honed to a minute. If you can't tell your story in a minute you aren't in touch with your most important, relatable details. You also probably haven't spent enough time reflecting on how powerfully the Holy Spirit has changed your life. By keeping it brief you allow your listener the chance to engage with your story. Hopefully, they will ask a few follow-up questions. If you drone on too long, they won't dare ask another question.

In my encounter with the reporter, I simply shared a 30-second version of how I had wrestled with the intellectual viability of the Christian faith. That was all it took to give my new friend permission to move beyond his intellect to his heart. I wanted to allow the Spirit to work. By not coming on too strong it allows space for your listeners to want to hear more. Trust the process.[7]

The only thing worse than an unfocused story is a long story that never gets to the point. Without the life change element, there's no purpose in sharing a spiritual story. There needs to be one clear plot line. That is,

7Hybels, Bill, Just Walk Across the Room: Simple Steps Pointing People to Faith (Grand Rapids:Zondervan) 2006 p 120

"When did your life change?" Any details you share must center on when your life changed. Remember to include the essential three points from the earlier exercise:

1. My life before Jesus;
2. When I met Jesus; and
3. How I've changed since meeting Jesus.

I regularly ask Christ followers to tell me their story. It is common to receive a list of irrelevant names, book titles, and run-on experiences unconnected to their life change. Or they name Christian events they attended that put a quiver in their liver. Or isles they have walked. Visions they've had. Weird dreams they remember. You get the idea.

Mistake #3
RECOUNTING OUR PAST SINS
AND ADVENTURES

Please don't recite for me the volume of sin you collected before you came to Christ. I don't care how good you were at sinning. I hear testimonies so focused on past sins that they become commercials for debauchery. Some people almost sound disappointed that they were rescued from their sin sick condition. That kind of story actually sounds like a sell job for how much fun is sin. It usually concludes with a brief wrap-up phrase like, "And I gave my life to Christ and the rest is history."

Mistake #4
THE FACT CHECKER

The fact checker goes like this: I began to think about spiritual things during my sophomore year in college. Or was it my freshman year? No, I think it was the summer between my freshman and sophomore year.

Who cares? Learn to tell your story with minimal minutia. Your story will gain power when you keep out of the weeds of trivial details.

MISTAKE #5
SPIRITUAL ARROGANCE

This may be the most repulsive card to play. The spiritual arrogance card usually carries with it a strong dose of legalistic fervor. If you want permanently to repel a person from the things of God, apply a dose of condemnation with spiritual arrogance. I believe the "tolerance" movement emerged as a response to Christians playing this card.

The secular push back from our culture comes from negative evangelistic strategies of the past. You've probably been in situations where a well-meaning church person is trying to evangelize you without knowing if you are a Christ-follower. They sprinkle a dose of pious remarks into their mix of condescending assumptions. It is quickly apparent they don't really care about you. Their primary concern is to let you know they have their stuff together. They genuinely believe they are doing this for your benefit. This is their way of helping you get in touch with your sinfulness. This is step one for them to lead you to Christ.[8]

I agree that repentance doesn't occur without an awareness of our sinful condition. But, the conversational

---

[8] Ibid., p 121

environment has changed. Things we could say in the past will no longer be tolerated.

Mistake #6
THE SELF OBSESSED STORY

This unfocused person takes you on a detail-laden stroll down Memory Lane. They want to turn the lights down, get out the slide projector and show you slides from their life, including family vacations and birthdays. Way too many details on things that don't matter.

We all need to sober up and realize that eternity hangs in the balance for the folks we are talking to. We need to get over ourselves and accept our responsibility to improve how we communicate our life change stories.

When you bog down in the details you alienate people. A secular person doesn't care. They don't relate to the fact that you were moved during the song "Tonight's the Night" at a Toby Mac concert. They don't know what a Toby Mac is. To them it sounds like a new sandwich at McDonalds.

Mistake #7
EXHAUSTING Insider LANGUAGE

Do you brew a lethal combination of self-obsession with exhausting insider language? Do you speak the language of the church, using vocabulary common to Christians, but mere mumbo jumbo to anyone outside the circle? When working on your story, try to eliminate any details that include church services, pastors names, the church you were attending at the time, or events with commonly known speakers or musical artists. This single step will make your story far more relatable.

I heard a guy share his story this way: "I recently went to a conference, the place was packed. I have never seen so many brothers and sisters in one place. Judah Smith spoke. He has written an amazing new book. Anyway, Judah gave an altar call after a cool concert on the last night of the conference. The band was amazing. They played this song I hear all the time on K-Love. That night I felt the conviction of the Spirit like never before. I had been running from the Lord. I admit it. I was backslidden. Man, the Spirit was moving that night in a mighty way.

"Anyway, the speaker said anyone who wants to get saved should come to the front. So I went down and got in this long line at the altar, and that night I accepted Jesus into my heart. Now He is my personal Lord and Savior. That was a great night, one I'll never forget. You should go with me next year, hopefully it won't be so hot."

Do you think he could have tightened up his story by sharing some relatable details, and avoiding the rambling details and insider language?

He could have said, "I had been living my life on my terms, and I was in a spiral of chaos and confusion that was taking me down. I heard a guy share that I didn't have to live that way, and he told me how I could live differently. That message struck a chord deep inside me. I realized I could live a life with purpose and meaning. I took the first step toward Christ that night and my life has been dramatically changed since."

Most of the phrases that were used in the first story mean very little to people outside of the Christian culture. When you bog down in the details you alienate most secular people. A secular person doesn't care. They don't care that you were moved during the song "Tonights the Night." They don't care that you had an encounter with the Holy Spirit during the last night of a too hot summer youth camp. It is far more powerful to say, "I heard a guy talk about how he had been a self obsessed jerk who thought the world revolved around him. That story really made me start thinking about my life."

I listen to countless stories that sound like they are being told in God code. It's almost like we want to confuse those who are outside of our culture. It will take effort to learn to speak in a way that will be relatable. Christian culture has developed an insider language that alienates us from a secular world. Learning to eliminate insider jargon from your story takes practice. Try looking at your story through the lens of your most pagan friend.

MISTAKE #8
PROXY WARS

When the topic of faith gets too contentious, the conversation often goes in a direction that can be destructive. Rather than engaging in a meaningful discourse, often the conversation devolves to "proxy wars". This happens when we debate peripheral issues. It's tempting to air grievances over hot button issues.

On a regular basis I do a motivation check. When I feel energized about a topic, I ask myself, "is this passion motivated out of love for the person, or am I wanting to win a debate"? If I can't answer yes, when I evaluate the situation I will ask the Spirit to correct my attitude. A spirit of vindication or correction will never produce spiritual fruit. It takes restraint to avoid getting sucked into non-essentials.

When Jesus engaged in a heated topic, it says, "He looked at him and loved him" (Mark 10:21). If we will trust the Spirit, we can intentionally love a person with whom we are in a tense conversation.

Too often I shift the motivation to serve my interest instead of benefiting the person far from Christ. When I want to win the debate, or prove that I am right, I have been ambushed by the "proxy war" mistake.

MISTAKE #9
NOT FOLLOWING THE
LEADING OF THE HOLY SPIRIT

So much of this process is uncharted and unfamiliar. The process of crucial conversations is not all that complicated when we remember to be led by the Holy Spirit. It all begins at a basic level. It begins with slowing down the RPMs of my life engine and looking to see who the Father has placed around me.

Then when I see a person standing alone across the room, looking at his phone, I take a breath, walk up to them and simply said, "Hi I'm Dan." I can't tell you how many times that results in an amazing crucial conversation. The basic element of a spiritual conversation begins with just being human. And from that point, allowing the Spirit to reveal the door you are to walk through.

When I allow myself to slow down and be "in step with the Spirit," I almost always find I am surrounded by powerful spiritual conversations. It is electrifying to be used to speak a word of encouragement to someone. It is amazing to be a tool in the hand of the Father.

It is thrilling to have the Spirit of God lead you into a conversation He has prepared for you. We have the privilege of watching the Father work to transform the life of an ordinary person. When I am prompted to reach out my hand and say, "Hi I'm Dan," I take the risk of stepping into a place of uncertainty. I am willing to take that risk because the Father often uses it to make a connection that would otherwise not happen. God often rewards this simple act of obedience in ways that overwhelm me.

When I first began this journey into Spiritual Conversations I was bold and undiscerning. I would talk with anyone who would listen. I exuberantly shared with anyone about the workings of the Spirit in my life. The only problem with my approach was I didn't realize that the power of my story was the work of the Spirit. Most of the time I was not following the lead of the Spirit. I was like many new followers of Christ, acting from my passion before it was linked with the gentle leading of the Spirit.

I have grown to realize that anything I do that doesn't come from keeping in step with the Spirit will not produce much fruit. Each morning before my feet hit the floor, I start my day saying, "Father, I can't make it today without your leading. Show me how to take this first step this morning with the power of your Spirit."

In this prayer time, I usually ask for discernment to find a disciple-able person with whom I can connect. I will often ask for clarity and discernment to know if I should speak or offer a loving act of servanthood instead. This is an adventure of keeping "in step with the Spirit."

Whether I engage in a spiritual conversation or an act of servanthood, I want my life to point to the one who has changed its direction. My loving Heavenly Father reached down into my condition and pulled me out of despair. God created me with a purpose in mind. He has placed His Spirit in me to prompt me to listen, love and serve the needs of those He is drawing to Himself.

Finding words adequately to define how we understand and grow in our relationship with the Holy Spirit is no simple task. Learning to listen to and follow the Spirit can seem foreign, mystical, even other worldly. It's hard to wrap our heads around how this works.

Every Christ follower knows it's real, even if it feels foreign. In fact, this process of listening to and following the Spirit actually connects us to the life and experience of those who followed the rabbi Jesus in Israel 2,000 years ago. Jesus sent the Spirit of God to comfort all who would open their lives to Him.

Jesus ended His time on earth by prophesying that we would, "Receive power when the Holy Spirit comes on you." The mission He tasked us with will be unlike anything else we ever will do. Jesus knew it would require Him to provide a source of supernatural power to help us. In John 20:21 Jesus empowered his followers with the single most powerful tool they would need. He said, "As the Father has sent me, I am sending you." And with that he breathed on them and said, "Receive the Holy Spirit."

In Galatians 5:25, Paul instructs new followers to "keep in step with the Spirit." In other words, the new believers were initially taught to associate life in the Spirit with the basic process of taking a step. The Spirit was given to us to accompany us on every step of our life journey. He encourages us to invite the Spirit into the dailiness of life. If we have access to the vast power of the Spirit living inside of us. then why would we not act on the guidance, motivation, and inspiration he offers?

I have found that when my relationship with Jesus is firing on all cylinders, I have a vibrancy in my thinking and sensitivity to the promptings of His Spirit. The idea of walking in step with the Spirit means that I will be attuned to the Spirit. I almost always have an increased awareness of things going on around me. It is almost as if all my senses are expanded. Life seems to slow down and I am able to see people and situations differently than I normally would. It is as if I have been given an assignment to discover disciple-able people who are searching for the Spirit of God, and I am given eyes to identify them.

When I am "in step with the Spirit," I can listen more keenly to the Spirit's gentle whisper. My spiritual senses would other wise be dulled to the signals of open, disciple-able people. When I am in step with the Spirit I can be incredibly alert to the Father arranging a spiritual conversation for me. On the other hand when I am distracted or overwhelmed I tend to be unaware of the needs of those around me – a condition in which I have spent too much of my life.

WHEN YOU BLOW IT

BRAIN TWEAK
A New Approach

Lets face it. It won't be long until you walk away from a conversation, and you know you've blow it. When you realize you've made a crucial conversation blunder, you now have the best opening line you'll ever have. Start by apologizing. I find my non-Christian friends begin to trust me when I admit to them I don't have it all figured out. Just say, "You know, last time we were together something you said really impacted me. I have not been able to get it out of my head. I guess I got so excited that I pushed too hard. You really matter to me as a friend, and I just wanted to say I am sorry that I pushed so hard last time. I kind of get all excited when I tell my God story."

Just admit it if you have made a gaff when you tried to have a spiritual conversation. Go quickly to the person and talk honestly. Just tell them you tried too hard, but that you care and you don't ever want to do anything that would violate their trust or harm your friendship.

Or you could say, "I know that what I shared put pressure on you and I never intended that." Another thing you could say is, "What I shared last time we talked was confusing, I guess I haven't thought deeply enough through something that has so rocked my world. I heard myself and I was offended at how arrogant I sounded. I am in a detox phase from all my church baggage. Please forgive me."

Most likely your gaff will come from one of the seven common mistakes listed above. Or you have reverted to some old school Christian approaches like pressuring someone to cross the line of faith when they weren't ready. Just take responsibility for the blooper and watch it open doors for real crucial conversations.

THE DO VERSUS DONE ICON

ICONTOOL BOX
Do Versus Done

This Icon is simple to use. If you find that you are mistake prone, this tool will help you avoid some of the previously mentioned pitfalls It is designed to help you share your story in the most simple way. The Do versus Done Icon allows you to contrast the tension between behavioral performance and the gift of salvation found in Jesus. It begins by pointing out that religion is spelled D-O. All religions are about learning and trying to DO enough to appease a god who has a voracious moral and behavioral appetite. The trouble is we will never know how we are doing in the DO column.

I explain to people who feel they are on the Eternal Reward Points Plan that the pressure to perform is common. I approach this icon from the point of confessing my failure at moral perfection. When we speak confessionally, others more readily embrace the concept.

Let's face it, every one of us has struggled with living on the DO side of the equation. You may confess that when you were bound up with a DO way of living you were a prisoner of religion. It is not uncommon to have someone tell you they're not a "church person." We must try to help them understand that a relationship with Christ and being in a church are separate things. The DO plan insidiously bores into our brain fueled as much from our upbringing, as from our church experience. Living a DO life centers on good moral performance and righteous actions. It's all about whether you DO enough right things to earn God's favor, to get into God's good graces. You have to learn, DO, strive and clean up your act to earn the required Eternal Reward Points to make it to Heaven. This icon addresses the mistaken belief that God is all about rewarding good moral behavior.

If the person seems to have a high sense of condemnation and guilt, you can explain that Jesus came to set us free from the pressure to DO more to please God. This sets Christianity apart from other religions. Romans 6:23 breaks down the DO versus DONE tension. It says,

"For the wages of sin is death, but the gift of God is eternal life in[b] Christ Jesus…"

Many people try to climb enough steps to reach God, weighed down by a back-pack full of fear, self doubt, fatigue and confusion. They worry that God is keeping a stat sheet or box score and they have little hope of ever achieving a wining score. So, people live in fear that they are falling short of the mysterious DO goal.

When using this icon, make the contrast between DO and DONE. It comes into focus when you surrender your life to Jesus. Only then can you drop your heavy backpack. He marked your account D-O-N-E. Jesus has D-O-N-E what you could never do through your feeble attempts to be moral. He set things straight. He paid for all the wrong stuff you ever did. Imagine that the Father has provided a vehicle to take you where you could never go on your own power. The vehicle of Christ work is like an airplane that puts you on the D-O-N-E side of the equation. The work has been done for you, and is able to lift you to a place you could never climb on your own.

What Christ did on the cross is spelled D O N E. It is enough. Jesus has done all that is necessary for us to be connected to the Father. The idea of Do VS Done can help you contrast the difference between our moral achievement and the core message of the Gospel It's not enough to understand this concept intellectually. We have to receive what He did for us on the cross. Jesus uniquely satisfied God's requirement for a perfect sacrifice to take care of our past, present, and future sin.

I suggest that you sketch out the idea as you explain, "This does so much more than put us 'in God's good graces.' You are given a life coach who will come to live inside of you. He will guide you through the process that will completely renew you. Because of what Christ did on the cross, your sins can be forgiven and you can find favor with the Father."

The point is not to memorize DO versus DONE as a formula, but to become so comfortable with it that you can:

- use it as a tool to walk through your story
- fill in the gaps, linger on conversational points
- help listeners identify with your story

The above description of DO vs DONE can help you remember where you are in the conversational flow. Remember all the icons are designed to be drawn on a napkin. If you don't want to do stick figure art, just write the two words: DO vs DONE.

This icon can be communicated as simply as writing those two little words on a slip of paper as you share how this has impacted you. It cements this powerful truth on a person's heart and mind. Be sure to discuss the contrast

Done
_____
Do

between the two ideas as you briefly share how you once were confused by the two approaches to life. Try to tighten your telling into a three minute window.

Occasionally, toss it back to them by asking, "Does this resonate with your experience and understanding?"[9]

(The do vs done icon idea was introduced in the 1950's, but was made popular by Bill Hybels in his book "Just Walk Across the Room")

---

[9] Ibid., page 137.

CRUCIAL QUESTIONS

CRUCIAL QUESTIONS
About Following Jesus

CRUCIAL QUESTIONS
RIGHT AND WRONG

- Do you think there are absolutes when it comes to right and wrong?

- How do/will you teach your kids right from wrong?

- Why do you think our culture has moved away from absolutes regarding right and wrong?

CRUCIAL QUESTIONS
MORALITY

- To what authority do you appeal?

- Do you believe God is concerned about our morality?

- Do you think discussions about doing right have a place in our culture?

crucial

conversations

CHANGE

HOW WE
CONNECT
WITH PEOPLE

SECTION 3

STORY OF NICODEMUS
JOHN 3:3-18

John 3:3 Now there was a Pharisee, a man named Nicodemus... He came to Jesus at night and said, "Rabbi, we know that you are a teacher who has come from God. For no one could perform the signs you are doing if God were not with him."

John 3:3 Jesus replied, "Very truly I tell you, no one can see the kingdom of God unless they are born again."

John 3:4 "How can someone be born when they are old?" Nicodemus asked. "Surely they cannot enter a second time into their mother's womb to be born!"

John 3:5 Jesus answered, "Very truly I tell you, no one can enter the kingdom of God unless they are born of water and the Spirit. Flesh gives birth to flesh, but the Spirit gives birth to spirit. You should not be surprised at my saying, 'You must be born again.' The wind blows wherever it pleases. You hear its sound, but you cannot tell where it comes from or where it is going. So it is with everyone born of the Spirit."

John 3:12-13 I have spoken to you of earthly things and you do not believe; how then will you believe if I speak of heavenly things? No one has ever gone into heaven except the one who came from heaven—the Son of Man.

John 3:16-18 For God so loved the world that he gave his one and only Son, that whoever believes in him shall not perish but have eternal life. For God did not send his Son into the world to condemn the world, but to save the world through him. Whoever believes in him is not condemned, but whoever does not believe stands condemned already

John 3:20 Everyone who does evil hates the light, and will not come into the light for fear that their deeds will be whoever lives by the truth comes into the light, so that it may be seen plainly that what they have done has been done in the sight of God.

"The 'show business,' which is so incorporated into our view of Christian work today, has caused us to drift far from Our Lord's conception of making disciples who make disciples."
- Oswald Chambers

"Jesus had no romantic notion of the cost of discipleship. He knew that following Him was as unsentimental as to be our commission, as demanding as love."
- Brennan Manning

CHAPTER 5

CRUCIAL CONVERSATIONS WITH A CULTURAL BELIEVER

This is Jesus' first trip to the city on the mountain since He went public as the Messiah. He introduces his wide-eyed back woods followers to the Holy City, Jerusalem. For His first act He goes head to head with the religious organized crime syndicate. After He puts the money changers on notice, he starts teaching and appears to announce something about the coming destruction of the temple building. He actually wraps that

announcement into a discussion about His coming
resurrection from the dead. Not a bad first day in the
Holy City, but He is not finished. He has a night
appointment that will become legendary.

CONVERSATION
Nick 'The Searcher'

The day's final meeting is with a
curious member of the Jewish high
court. Nicodemus is prosperous, devout and upstanding.
He's accustomed to rubbing shoulders with dignitaries.
He's not a fragile or emotional person. Nicodemus calls
Jesus "rabbi," a term of high respect. We know Jesus as a
poor carpenter with no formal academic training. At first
glance Nicodemus looks like a cultural believer who
follows the party line. Something else clearly is stirring
beneath the water line. Most cultural believers would not
be pursuing a deeper, more vibrant relationship with God
the Father. Most would be content to go through the
prescribed motions, staying content in their circles of
power and comfort.

The Spirit of God has moved Nicodemus to take a
massive risk, as he hungers for a more in-depth spiritual
conversation – evidenced by his humble and open
minded approach.

Nick begins with a curious but courteous intro:
"Pardon me, Rabbi, I've heard many wonderful things
about you. You obviously are a teacher who has been sent
from God."

Nick is probably thinking, "I could lose everything
if I am found talking with you. That is why I would prefer
to meet under the cover of darkness." Nick had a lot to

lose by meeting with Jesus. He was neck deep in the corrupt religious syndicate. "Yet there is something about you that draws me, I can't quite explain it."

He follows this by saying, "People have been talking about the miracles you do. They give you a great deal of credibility." But Jesus turns the conversation on a dime and interrupts Nick to say, "You must be born again." In no other conversation does Jesus take such a hard pivot. Jesus intentionally pushes his buttons. Nick intended to approach Jesus the way he'd been trained as a student of the law. He knows that when you approach a rabbi you need to have a good question in your pocket. Jesus' bold words must have startled him and seemed to be a strange pronouncement. This will not be a theological dialogue if Jesus can help it.

BRAIN TWEAK
Born Again Conversation

"Born again." That has become a loaded term, especially as outspoken Christian President Jimmy Carter introduced it more broadly to the public world-wide. How does one become "born-again" anyway? The moniker "born-again Christian" carries a heavy stigma these days. Being born again has been associated with hard right politics and legalistic judgmental thinking. Most people today aren't drawn to the term. Jesus used this phrase to prompt some "out-of-the box thinking" in Nick.

Jesus targets any hint of self-righteous piety in Nick, using a metaphor of birth. Jesus asks, in effect, how integral was your participation in the act of your birth? What was required of you? Did you work hard to earn the privilege of being born? What skill set was required? You were barely necessary. You don't earn or contribute anything to being born. Jesus is saying, Nick, birth is a free gift. And so it is with the spiritual birth. You are born into this new Kingdom by grace. No moral piety or religious performance is necessary.

Nick began to talk to Jesus about church leadership and positional authority. Jesus immediately turned the conversation to what it would look like for Nick to be spiritually born. This conversation pivoted from theoretical to practical in an instant.

Jesus explained that it is impossible to see and understand the kingdom of God unless a spiritual birth takes place.

> *"I tell you, no one can see the kingdom of God unless they are born again."*   -John 3:3

A common misreading of this passage leads to conversations about going to Heaven when we die. That is not what this crucial conversation is about. This conversation is about a cultural believer who thinks he understands what the Father is up to. Jesus shows the religious expert that he must reset how he thinks about everything.

You must have such a hard reset it will be as if you're starting over. This new life will enable you to see the new Kingdom in your midst. Jesus spoke of this new Kingdom in non-earthly terms, yet it is immediately present. This is not some distant future Kingdom.

Jesus proclaimed, "The Kingdom of God is in your midst" (Luke 17:21). It's not a distant future thing. Jesus taught that the Kingdom was so close the defining event would happen before the next meal.

> *For I tell you I will not drink again from the fruit of the vine until the kingdom of God comes." -Luke 22:18*

Jesus was not inviting Nick to seek a "pie in the sky, by and by" kind of Kingdom. It was right before his eyes if he would just open them and be "born again."

After Jesus calls for a total restart, the camera pans back to Nick, who is now hung up on the birth metaphor. He is now nearly 20 times the size he was at birth, and mom is getting up in years. He could not fathom how this would work.

> *"How can someone be born when they are old? Nicodemus asked. Surely they cannot enter a second time into their mother's womb to be born!"*
> *- John 3:4*

Jesus clears up the mom question by sticking with the birth metaphor.

> *"Jesus answered, 'Very truly I tell you, no one can enter the kingdom of God unless they are born of water and the Spirit.'"*   *-John 3:5*

Those who listened closely figured out that Jesus used the water birth as a metaphor for the physical birth that begins with a gush. Now He depicts the birth in the Spirit as only being sourced from the Spirit of God.

> *"Flesh gives birth to flesh, but the Spirit gives birth to Spirit."*   *- John 3:6*

In one paragraph Jesus changes everything. Everyone needs two birth events: their physical birth and their spiritual birth. The physical birth gets the ball rolling, but it cannot answer life's great questions. You need the second birth to be complete. This was a new concept. Jesus gave the world a new paradigm for life. Nick could add nothing to this conversation. This expert in all things religious was standing before Jesus speechless.

This idea of a new spiritual start to life explains why the prostitutes and tax collectors flock after this Jesus guy. That group loved the idea that they could have a new life in the Father. Before this the only people who could reach the Father were those with the financial bandwidth to do religious pursuits. The hard scrabble life did not afford any margin to pursue religious piety. Plus, the religious bought their status with private school education and cultural influence. The fact that they could read the religious writings gave them great power in that society.

Jesus was announcing to Nick that the common person could now access the Father by being given a new start, a mulligan, a do-over. Nick, on the other hand, wasn't sure if he was ready to give up all he had worked for to this point in his life. He was not a down and outer. He had a rabbinic education, he had the wealth to pursue religion and piety.

The idea of a re-start can be attractive when you are a prostitute, an outcast, or backed into a corner. When you are a part of the corrupt establishment like

Nicodemus a re-start could cost you influence and position.

Jesus was saying in effect that Nicodemus had invested everything into a system that ultimately could never reward him for his high devotion. Jesus was saying everyone has to start at the same place – they must be born spiritually to be a part of His new kingdom. This hard reset at first blush looked like loss for a man who had invested everything into an airtight religious system. The born again idea Jesus proposed, is far more revolutionary than most of us realize.

It's as if Jesus just announced a spiritual currency shift. Jesus is shifting away from all the religious elite had known and promoted. He was in effect saying, "All you have invested in and trusted in the past is not currency the Father accepts."

Civil war currency

BRAIN TWEAK
Kingdom Currency

After the Civil War those who held confederate currency had a set number of days to redeem it for federal dollars. After that, the confederate currency would be worthless.

Jesus just told Nicodemus, all the moral currency he'd been hoarding was worthless in the new kingdom. He's been banking on moral achievement to create spiritual wealth. He's been investing in a currency that will soon be worthless. The gold standard for the new currency is trust and confidence in Jesus, and the work of the Spirit. Jesus continues to explain,

"The wind blows…You hear its sound, but you cannot tell where it comes from… So it is with everyone born of the Spirit." -John 3:8

Jesus admits that it can be difficult to trust in something that seems intangible. He reminds us that we accept the wind is real. We have never seen the wind, but everyone believes it exists. We have all witnessed how it blows through the leaves on the trees.

When the Spirit of God blows through the life of a person you see its impact in their life. We know the Spirit is real even though we have never seen the wind. You have only seen the effect of the wind. When a person embraces Jesus we see the impact of that relationship.

Jesus created a currency shift. He introduced Nicodemus to how this new economy functions. This is not a shift of moral behavior, or piety, or new codes and customs. It is a shift that invites us to come alive to the work of the Spirit and to be born in a way that embraces a personal relationship with the Father.

This new shift can be confusing because religious people use a great deal of God talk. Moralists trust their own goodness, while talking about God. Legalists trust their ability to navigate loopholes, while talking about God. Pietists trust their ability to observe religious traditions, while talking about God. Christ followers trust Jesus and grow to better understand who the Father is.

At first the shifts are subtle and easily missed by the undiscerning eye. Most religionists aren't even aware that the more they trust in moral behavior, the less they trust in God. The more they trust in religious loopholes, the less they trust in God. The more they trust in religious traditions, the less they trust in God. Their actions say, why trust in God when they can trust in their own goodness, loopholes, or piety?

Sin happens when we look beyond God for our salvation. Sin is putting yourself in the place of God, becoming your own savior and lord. The First Commandment gives the biblical definition of sin. Anything in our life that takes the place of God is sin. The morally good person who is not religious is no worse than the highly religious person who trusts in his moral goodness. Both are their own god and have no room for the transformation the Spirit brings, or the person and work of Jesus.

THE WIND OF THE SPIRIT WAS BLOWING

It was a sunny, warm Saturday in Myrtle Beach. The Christian band Mercy Me had just wrapped up their concert. Our church had helped sponsor a free outdoor event one street from the ocean.

Now that the event was over, a great deal of work lay before us. We had to break everything down and haul it away. It is easy to miss the crucial conversation opportunities that lay ahead when we are distracted or under pressure. How easy it is just to meet obligations and operate on autopilot.

There had been a great deal of prayer around this event. Our church had taken on a large expense and we had high expectations that the Father would give us opportunities to engage in crucial conversations with concert goers. How many times have Christians produced an event hoping that the event itself will have some intrinsic value? I reminded our team that the value of this event was to build relationships with people we might eventually be able to disciple. Jesus seemed to use events to engage the crowd, as a step toward identifying new disciples. We were hoping to do the same.

We invested a great deal of intentional time and training. We spent time preparing our team to have crucial conversations. I reminded them that the value of the event would be reduced to a free concert, if we weren't ready to meet those the Father had brought to the event.

Before this event I prayed, "Father give me eyes to see what you see. Give me antennas to detect your Spirit's movement. Help me to know where I need to be sensitive. I want to be led by you today."

I had several conversations but nothing much happened yet. The band wrapped up. The speaker made his final remarks, and we were preparing to break down the stage when a middle-aged man caught my eye. He was by himself, sitting on the ground while everyone else was preparing to exit. I introduced myself and sat down beside him.

I thanked him for coming. He said he enjoyed the music. He had been stressed and was at the beach to get away for a couple of days for some rest and relaxation. That's a common prescription for beach visitors. Then I asked a direct question. "You said you've been under a lot

of stress lately. What's been going on in your life?" He
brushed aside my question with a superficial response.
Ok, I had followed up, and this guy is giving me nothing.
I was about to bail and get back to work. It looked like
this would be just a polite superficial conversation that
would go nowhere.

Fortunately, the Spirit was at work in ways that I
could not see. He was inviting me to participate with Him
on behalf of my new friend.

I had a strange prompting from the Spirit to share a
phrase from my quiet time that morning, it came from the
Nicodemus story. The entire time we had been talking the
Spirit had been pressing me to bring up the verse where
Jesus said,

> "The wind blows… You hear its sound, but you
> cannot tell where it comes from… So it is with
> everyone born of the Spirit."   -John 3:7-8

I couldn't shake this passage or the Spirit's
prompting. I wanted to work it in without being weird. I
was torn between obeying and being a normal polite
superficial conversationalist. So I pressed in. I said, "One
phrase that you said, stood out to me. You mentioned
earlier that you just happened to stop by today. Tell me
about that." He said, "I heard the music and came over."
This was a dead end. He was giving me one phrase
answers.

The Spirit was prompting me to give it one more
try. I decided to go for the deep end of the conversation. I
sensed that the Spirit was prompting this way, all the time
hoping this wouldn't be a belly flop. I said, "I have been

gripped by how the Father brings people to events like this one. You mentioned that you just happened to stop by. I am glad you did. I was just this morning reading something where Jesus said, "Our lives are spiritually influenced by the Father. He blows people and events into our lives that influence us. The Bible says it works like the wind. We never see the wind, yet we all know it exists. The work of God is like that in our lives."

"This concert may be like that," I said. "In fact, I have found in my life that God's influence is a like a wind. The Father is present even though He can't be seen. I know I am influenced by the unseen, loving hand of the Father. I find that He desperately wants to connect with us. It sounds like you probably didn't anticipate coming tonight, but you are here. Do you think perhaps the Spirit of God has blown into your life and brought you here tonight for a reason?"

He lay down face first in the sand and began to weep. I don't mean he was sniffling. He was sobbing and violently shaking. I didn't know what I had done, or how to appropriately respond. I put my hand on his shoulder, perhaps to comfort him, or maybe to give me something to do while I sat by the sobbing stranger. I had never had anyone respond that way to something I had been prompted to say. After what seemed like 45 minutes, but was probably about forty-five seconds, he sat up, collected himself and apologized.

Then he said, "Do you recognize me?" I admitted I did not have a clue. He told me his name, then paused like I should recognize him. He said, "I am the guy in the news." That still didn't give me a clue, so he told me his story. I am the Philadelphia lawyer in the news. He began to unpack his story. He was like Nicodemus, this man spent his life thinking he was good with God because he studied religion and had lived according to his personal moral code. All the while, he was working in a corrupt system. He had taken it farther than Nicodemus. He was a lawyer for the Mafia. He had taken on a very famous crime boss as a client many years ago.

He said the money was too good to pass up. This kind of money would pay for his five kids' college and he convinced himself that representing the mob would take care of his needs for life. The East coast crime family he was working for had removed the Gambino mob in a bloody exchange years before.

I was familiar with the crime family he represented from the A&E reality show that bore their name. It was a show about this modern day crime syndicate and their mafia lifestyle. The lawyer had been made a very wealthy man by the mob boss. My new friend had won multiple court cases that allowed "The Don" to remain a free man. He explained that the FBI finally convicted "The Don" after proving he used chemicals in his basement to dissolve the body of a man he had murdered. Many TV shows have been based on this wicked story.

Once the FBI took down the "family", they went after my sobbing new friend. They had gotten him disbarred so he could no longer practice law. They seized his property. His wife left him and took their children. As we talked, the real story emerged. He had borrowed a friend's vehicle and penthouse at the beach. All the while he was there, he was considering ways to take his life. He had decided to jump off of the 21st floor of the hotel across the street.

He had enough whisky to provide the courage to leap. He had a gun in the room. Just an hour earlier he was preparing to start drinking to gather the courage to either squeeze the trigger or take the leap from the penthouse. Before he took the first drink, he heard a pounding on the ocean front sliding glass door of his room. It sounded like someone beating on the glass. The wind seemed to be trying to get his attention.

He finally opened the door to make sure someone wasn't pounding on the glass. When he did he heard the music from the concert just before the speaker gave a brief invitation. The speaker said, "If you need a new start in life come to the stage. We would love to talk with you."

So this broken man began to walk in the direction of the music as the band played its last song. That is when he met me. He said. "It was like God was speaking through whoever it was, but they had the perfect message to get my attention. As I was walking over here, I was praying, 'God if you are real prove yourself to me now before I take my life." That is when I met you.

I shared with him how Christ could change his life. I asked him if he was ready to make the shift in his life to follow Christ and become a disciple. He said he had never been told that Jesus longs to care for and lead us through whatever mess we are in. He was ready to take the next step.

He began the journey that day. He faced a lot of challenges — one of them was the next week when he was sentenced to a lengthy prison term. We stayed in contact and we were able to do some discipleship development even though a great many hurdles littered his path.

Crucial Questions

CRUCIAL QUESTIONS
About Following Jesus

CRUCIAL QUESTIONS
TALKING ABOUT NEW BIRTH

•What do you think of when someone uses the phrase "born again?"

•Why do you think it has that connotation?

•Have you ever wished you could get a mulligan (do over)? What would you do differently with your life?

•Have you ever had anyone approach you and try to talk to you about God? How did you feel after the encounter?

•If someone wanted to talk to you about God, how would you like to be approached?

"Those who aren't following Jesus aren't His followers. It's that simple. Followers follow, and those who don't follow, aren't followers."

— **Scott McKnight,**

"You will know as much of God, and only as much of God, as you are willing to put into practice."

— **Eric Liddell**

CHAPTER 6

CRUCIAL CONVERSATIONS WITH A CHRISTIAN (*!@#%)

Amy was a 33-year-old personal trainer. Her first words when I met her were, "I've come to realize that I'm a Christian bitch." Wow, that was not how I expected this conversation to start. This fit, confident young woman admitted that even though she had spent her life doing all the right things, something was amiss.

"I've grown up in the church," she said. "I know all the right answers, but I've destroyed my life. For six years of marriage, I had to have it my way. To have things not go my way produced a kind of panic in me. I felt out of control."

Her honesty bled out in a way that I suspected felt freeing, yet unnerving. She continued, "I was in the middle of facing my greatest life test. My world was falling apart. My marriage had stress fractures. I couldn't sleep. I was depressed. I felt like my life had speed wobbles. I had pushed as far as I could and the wheels were about to come off.

 **EXAMPLE**
Conception/Birth: "After church, one Sunday, another mom struck up a conversation with me in the hallway of the children's wing. She invited me to meet for coffee. We got together over several weeks. Her name was Katie and she asked me several questions that got me thinking. I began to take a hard look at who I had become. I had become a demanding, unhappy woman who was hard to live with. All the while I thought I had God figured out. I knew the right 'church' answers. I had gone from Christian school and youth group to a Christian college and then to a Christian marriage. I had been baptized at nine. I had always been a good girl, and done the church thing. But I was empty inside.

I was miserable and I made my husband miserable. I was spending money and driving us into debt. To make things worse, I developed a drinking problem. I rationalized an affair was no big deal because my husband wasn't meeting my needs. It all came collapsing down. I have been living a double life."

Amy put her head in her hands and began to weep. It was no surprise to me that Katie had built a relationship with her. Katie was part of a group learning how to have effective crucial conversations. I selected Katie because she cared for others and had been radically impacted by the work of Christ in her life. She recently told me she was praying for Amy and was looking for a chance to have a crucial conversation with her with the hope of cultivating her as a new disciple.

Amy described how Katie had connected with her. Katie did a great job of just loving her the way she was. She didn't correct her, or judge her, she just listened, asked questions and shared her own story. There were plenty of parallels between the two women. Amy described how Katie had drawn a diagram that really helped her. On one side it said *conception*, and on the other it said *birth*.

Katie admitted that she had wrestled with some of the same questions haunting Amy. She had been baptized as a child and was involved in church. Katie shared how it took some time for her to realize she had not really surrendered to Christ. Katie admitted to Amy that she too had made promises, cut divine bargains, and prayed only when things got tough. She realized she was living as a practical atheist – someone who claims to be a Christian, but lives so worldly it would appear they don't believe God is real. Katie shared how she had been spiritually conceived but not born.

She had a form of spiritual life, Katie said, but it was far from what the Father intended for her. She was stuck at conception. Her previous pastor consoled her, convincing her she was an average church member. He reviewed the details of her spiritual life. "You have been saved – check, you've been baptized – check, you're in a small group – check. Perhaps you just need to double down on your commitment to Jesus. Perhaps you should rededicate your life. Don't worry you are a Christian," the pastor told Katie.

But Katie hungered for more. She prayed, attended church, and occasionally read her Bible. She did church sponsored acts of kindness and went on mission trips. But something was still missing.

Like a baby in the womb there was life but not the full freedom of which she heard others speak. Katie told Amy how she finally surrendered to Christ as an adult. This spiritual awakening shook her to her core. After that season she experienced a new peace, joy, and hope. She had a new gear to love others, and the ability to be genuinely kind.

Katie asked Amy if she had ever had a time in her adult life when she hungered to know Christ more. Exasperated, Amy said she had tried to get closer to Jesus but just didn't know how. She was afraid she was beyond hope. Was it possible for her to break free from the cycle she was stuck in?

Then Amy told me how Katie took a napkin and began to draw a diagram and share more of her story.

Katie drew two poles.

One said *conception*, the other said *birth*. She explained how she had been spiritually conceived when she was a little girl, but didn't experience spiritual birth until she was an adult.

Conception   Birth

She asked Amy where she thought she was on this scale.

Amy said, "I know I had a conception experience when I was a child. I was somewhere on the conception side of birth." Amy said she placed an X just inside the birth line.

"It was then I realized I had always called myself a Christian," Amy said. "I had regularly taken steps to rededicate my life, or somehow re-commit myself to being a better Christian. All along I had been cutting deals with God so I could live my life the way I wanted. I had no idea I had become a 'committed' cultural Christian bitch."

Amy admitted to Katie that she'd never had a genuine surrender moment. She spent the next two days thinking about the conversation. Eventually she called Katie and confessed that her story had made an impression on her. She knew something had to change.

That day Amy took a step that opened up her life to the work of the Spirit in a way that was different from all previous attempts. She said, "For the first time, I'm experiencing what it means to have a new life."

Katie's crucial conversation with Amy led to genuine life change. That is the reason we take the risk to have these conversations. Before long Amy became a growing, reproducing disciple.

The old model of having evangelistic conversations designed to lead a person to Christ, and then abandon them, must be replaced. Our conversations must take the next step of discipleship. They need to parallel the conversations Jesus had. He spent time identifying people he could disciple. His goal was not to get them to pray a sinner's prayer. He wanted to grow reproducing disciples, not merely religious church people.

Jesus' secret sauce was knowing how to find the right people. He used crucial conversations to identify people to invest in. Katie engaged Amy in a crucial conversation by design. It wasn't long until she saw in Amy qualities she recognized from her own life. Katie took the step to share her story with Amy. The Holy Spirit used the encounter, and Amy became disciple-able. The key was for Katie to find the right person to invest in.

Conception Birth Icon

ICON TOOL BOX
Using The Icon

The icon Katie used was one that I taught in our crucial conversation training. This tool assists people in crucial conversations to tell their story. Learn to tell your story in a way that allows the other person to overhear the gospel. When this happens they will be invited to join you in identifying where they are in their spiritual journey.

**THE POWER OF THE ICON IS NOT IN THE ART.
IT'S IN THE HEART OF THE PASSAGE.**

When you draw this icon you will need to share your personal story like Katie did. With some practice you can learn to tell your life change story in a way that parallels the conversation Jesus had with Nicodemus.

It is essential that you base your personal story in the theme that Jesus created for Nicodemus. This will allow the other person to identify where they are in the conception-birth life cycle.

To use this icon effectively you must have a grasp of John 3:3-8. The Spirit uses the truth of scripture to change lives. When you're using the conception-birth icon it's important to be able to put the passage into your own words.

DRAWING THE
CONCEPTION BIRTH ICON

As you draw this icon briefly describe what your life was like in the days before you trusted Christ as your savior. Let this Icon be the basis of how you tell your life change story. Remember to include the following three core elements to your story.

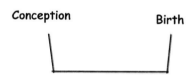

•*Before you met Christ.* What was your conception experience? Perhaps it happened when you were a child, and you began to think about who God is for the first time.

•*When you met Christ.* Briefly describe what happened to draw you to reflect on your life and to surrender control to Jesus.

•*After you met Christ.* Take some time to describe the change that transpired after surrendering to Christ. Your description will help a person who has not yet received the indwelling power of the Holy Spirit to understand life change.

The fruit of the Spirit is often the best descriptor of how the work of Christ changes a life. You might say something like:

"When I took the step to trust Jesus, I had a new surge of love for other people. I had a joy that was different from circumstantial happiness. I had a peace and patience that was uncharacteristic for me. All that because of this new birth transaction."

If you rewind from your spiritual birth moment you discover that often there was a season of gestation after spiritual conception. It could have been a time in childhood when we wrestled with spiritual thoughts between maybe ages six and twelve.

The autumn when I was about eleven was particularly monumental for me. The warm mountain nights were perfect for laying on the balcony of our house, which overlooked Green River. There was not another house within sight. I remember watching the spectacular meteor showers that year. I just knew I was not a result of the random forces of evolution, as my text books said. I knew God had created me. That season put me on a quest to know more about my creator.

I believe every young person wrestles with crucial spiritual questions around this age. It is a natural time of curiosity. Romans 1:19-20 tells us:

"Since what may be known about God is plain to them, because God has made it plain to them. For since the creation of the world God's invisible qualities — his eternal power and divine nature — have been clearly seen, being understood from what has been created, so that people are without excuse."

Virtually everyone muses about their creation and purpose. But this season of spiritual conception does not guarantee there will be a spiritual awakening moment. By drawing the icon as you describe your story, you can help the other person better diagnose where they are in the spiritual birth process.

The power of the icon comes when you ask the person to describe where they are in their journey of spiritual development. By handing them the pen, they have to assess for themselves where they are in the continuum. A person who claims himself a Christian will rethink the truth of his identity in light of how you have framed a person being "born again."

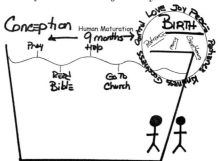

Defining a Christian life as embracing the "fruit of the Spirit" sheds new light. Consider the qualities that emerged when you had your spiritual eyes opened as a newly born follower. I will bet that you experienced for the first time the life giving qualities that emerged when the Spirit moved in. I know that I had a new sense of love for others, I was filled with joy, I had a peace like I had never known. There was patience in situations like never before. I had the capacity to slow down and be more kind. The descriptions can go on and on. This was the powerful working of the Holy Spirit in me. The power of this icon comes when you can describe the life change story that occurred when this transformation happened in you.

Every time I've used this icon, I've been surprised at how the Father assists the person to accurately assess their spiritual condition. Persons who have had an encounter with the Holy Spirit often quickly celebrate, and affirm that they can identify with your experience. There will be no escaping it if they have not yet known the work of the Spirit in a personal way. A person can't fake that level of transformation. Helping a person get an accurate grip on their spiritual condition can play a huge role in allowing the Father to move us forward. Several things can come from using this icon. It can assist a cultural Christian to:

- Determine for themselves if they have been spiritually conceived, but not yet born

- Do some spiritual assessment, reflection and evaluation

- Self-diagnose their spiritual condition

- Reflect on their spiritual receptivity

- Reflect on their need to have an adult encounter

The 11-year-old version of me did not understand how to follow Christ in the adult version of my life. I finally realized that I had to make an adult decision to surrender my life to the will and work of the Father.

When a person has a spiritual conception moment they are experiencing the initial spiritual awakening. This is a critical season for spiritual development. Nicodemus must have had a spiritual conception moment. Perhaps it was while he was staring into a starry Judean night. He was probably able to discern that he had been created for a purpose. He began to study and follow the ways of Judaism. Jesus insisted that he still lacked the adult experience of spiritual birth. He had to be "born again." It wasn't until he met the one who flung the stars into place that it all came together.

Neither a spiritual conception moment, nor feeling the weight of our sinful condition necessarily give way to a spiritual birth. Jesus guided Nicodemus through the process. He forced Nicodemus to reflect on the image of the wind. Had he seen the Spirit blow through the branches of his life? If the wind is blowing in your life it will leave evidence. The wind of the Spirit, too, will move you.

One of the trends in the Evangelical Church is the inclination to declare a person "saved" after an initial spiritual conception encounter. When an over zealous pastor or parent drives the potential new disciple to cap the spiritual birth process at the point of conception, the true "born again" experience often never happens. When a zealous pastor baptizes a naive child, the pastor is declaring the process complete, often at a surprisingly young age.

The only course of action will be for this young child to attempt to live the Christian life in his or her own power instead of being infused by the power of the Holy Spirit. This recipe creates cultural Christians. When we grow up in this culture we try unsuccessfully to live the Christian life in the power of the flesh and our earnest desire to live a moral life. In this case we have no ability to live a transformed life. We will not be able to reproduce other disciples. We have no life change story to share.

Too many simply accept "churchification" in the place of genuine life change. The potentially disciple-able person too often was rushed through the salvation process. When this happens they are thrust into the "churchification" process, only to be abandoned to survive in a foreign institution called the local church.

We do a person a huge disservice when we don't provide them a context that allows for natural spiritual development. Without development, the new birth experience can get wrapped around the axle of theology.

This can lead to an unnecessary conversation about the doctrine of the "security of the believer."

You also can use this icon to help a person understand if perhaps their Christian identity comes from some qualifying activity. Maybe they took a Catholic CCD class as a child, or accepted Jesus in their heart at five, and were baptized. Perhaps they responded to an altar call at summer camp. Often a person is proclaimed a "saved" Christian and baptized or celebrated in a formal-ceremonial way at such a point.

Maybe this is you, and you thought the next step was to act the part of a Christian. Too many times people like you were never encouraged to explore their newfound spiritual interest. Too many are never discipled again. They become victims of church malpractice.

Spiritual conception and spiritual birth are as different as natural conception and birth are different. This is why many of our evangelical churches have such a difficult time discipling and growing new converts.

No one knows immediately if a person who makes a spiritual response has been spiritually born. We will, however, _know in a year..._ let that sink in. Isn't it shocking to see the burst of growth in a newborn baby? In one year an infant grows from a messy, beautiful bundle to a walking, talking, functioning member of the family. The same is true for a person who has had a spiritual birth. They should experience a surge of new life that will propel them to a place of high spiritual function in the first year. If this hasn't happened we might want to share a spiritual birth story by using the conception-birth icon.

REVIEW HOW TO USE THE ICON

ICON TOOL BOX
The Power Of The Icon

The power of this icon rests in the description of what it means to be truly "born again." You'll need to be able to present your personal rebirth story.

- The presenter must describe how they have been transformed by the work of the Holy Spirit.

- Describe personally the fruit of the Spirit that has emerged in your life.

- Give practical descriptions of the joy and peace that took place when you embraced the person of the Holy Spirit.

- Encourage your listener to indicate where on the diagram they believe themselves to be. Would they be between conception and birth, or in the area of post birth? Hand your pen to the person, and ask them to place an "X" where they see themselves.

- No one knows if a person is "born" when they pray the prayer. We should know in a year!

- Help them determine their spiritual condition for themselves.

Too often we think about having crucial conversations only with those who are "living far from Christ". Conversations with cultural Christians are equally crucial. Jesus first connected with the culturally religious crowd. They were the ones who regularly engaged in conversations about spiritual topics. They were often closed minded to outside schools of thought. As a group they proved to be difficult to move in a positive direction. However, there were individuals who were spiritually open and disciple-able. Jesus first engaged Nicodemus in a spiritual conversation.

BRAIN TWEAK
Insiders need salvation too

Nicodemus, was an insider who needed salvation. In every church are those who need to engage in crucial conversations. We must not overlook this rich pool of disciple-able people under our noses. There is a reason Jesus engages Nicodemus in a crucial conversation early in the Kingdom movement. Jesus wants to include culturally Christian people in His Kingdom revolution.

Jesus cares for this religious man who lacks understanding of God's Kingdom even though Nicodemus has dedicated his life to all things religious. He is as far from the Kingdom as any prostitute or tax collector. He just doesn't know it. Remember, Jesus encountered two very similar people within 24 hours. One is an outsider and the other an insider. The Samaritan woman (the outsider) and Nicodemus (the insider) are in the same category, they are sinners in need of grace.

BRAIN TWEAK
Insiders & Outsiders

Church people trying to put God in their debt feel like insiders but have the same spiritual need as an outsider. Their fruitless religious efforts are like playing a game in which no one knows the rules or the score. That would be maddening and begs the question: "How do you tilt the universe in your favor?"

To one, Jesus offers living water and to the other he extends new birth. Both metaphors present the difference between life and death. Both people need to surrender to the one offering the gift of life. Jesus invites both to give up trying to be their own savior.

Crucial Questions

Crucial questions
spiritual conception

- Do you remember a time when as a child you asked your parents crucial questions about God?

- What kind of answers did you get?

- Do you think your parents ever wrestled with perplexing God questions?

- Have you ever wondered what it takes to make God pleased with you?

- Did you ever fear Heaven and Hell or the wrath of God?

Crucial questions
Who is God?

- Would God say you were for Him or against Him?

- What evidence do you use to prove your case?

- Have you ever second-guessed your view of God?

- If you could receive direct and immediate answers from God for any three questions, what would you ask?

CRUCIAL

"But in your hearts revere Christ as Lord. Always be prepared to give an answer to everyone who asks you to give the reason for the hope that you have."
– 1 Peter 3:15

"If you really believe in the redeeming and transforming power of God's presence in a person's life, the single greatest gift you can give someone is an explanation of how to be rightly connected to Him."
- Bill Hybels

CHAPTER 7

CRUCIAL CONVERSATIONS
THE POWER OF PISTEUO

The most misunderstood word in the Bible is the word that is translated "believe." The modern church has shouldered this word and carried it in the wrong direction. The Greek word creating the confusion is *pisteuo*. How is this simple word the source of so much misunderstanding?

An entire grass roots church culture mistakenly thinks that Jesus' use of the word believe/*pisteuo* means we should dispassionately repeat a set of sterile doctrines, theologies, and beliefs. The Greek word *pisteuo* is occasionally translated "faith," which creates less confusion. The word is most commonly translated in the New Testament as "believe" or "belief." *Pisteuo* or a variation of it appears 248 times in the New Testament. Most often it is spoken by Jesus. The word is central to understanding Jesus and the message of the gospel.

The English language doesn't have a single word that fully contains the concept Jesus intends. A better translation word would be "all in" or, "abandon all competing ways to live, and fully embrace the new Jesus Kingdom." See the dilemma? There is no simple way in English to communicate the idea Jesus has in mind.

Since the first translations were done *pisteuo* has been hijacked by entire theological systems. Debate devolved into single-minded discussions about right theology and doctrines. This was never Jesus' intention when he spoke about the power of being, "all in for His new transformational Kingdom." Because they misunderstand the word, most in the modern church aren't having crucial conversations that lead others to be all in and truly pisteuo. They are instead having conversations that center around debate or simply telling others to "believe" in Jesus like children "believe" in Santa Claus.

When Jesus used the word translated "believe," He never used it in a creedal or religious way. Jesus never invites us to "believe" a set of doctrines, or "believe" proper theology. Jesus never longed for his followers to become embroiled in tedious creedal debates, or endless dogmatic comparisons of doctrine. Jesus spoke a word that at its origin is passionately missional. Jesus said,

> *"For God so loved the world that he gave his one and only Son, that whoever would* **pisteuo/believe** *in him shall not perish but have eternal life."*   *- John 3 16*

Jesus demonstrated an entirely new level of intensity for what it means to be a disciple. Yet, the modern church has embraced the lie that it's a proper adherence to a right set of biblical concepts that makes us obedient disciples.

Imagine a high speed train crash in a treacherous mountain pass, leaving cars and passengers dangling over a 1,000-foot abyss. Rescue workers arrive ready to spring into action to save lives, but instead of initiating a rescue plan the leaders start a heated debate over the plan's proper wording. They break the team into groups to study the wording and wordsmith the dispatch document that drew them together. Before long this discussion has completely re-directed every minute aspect of the mission. In the process, rescue personnel with different expertise lobby for the wording to reflect their training. They want to be true to their specific tribe.

So the teams break into separate camps that reflect their perspective and affirm their beliefs. Meanwhile, the despairing passengers are forgotten.

The rescue team lost its focus of what matters most. They abandoned the mission to argue over secondary issues. Like the rescue team, we have a massive problem.

The church has lost sight of the *pisteuo* mission to which Jesus called us.

Our misunderstanding of this word is at the heart of the mission problem in the American Church. We have invested – dare I say wasted – some of our best energies on the nuances of right belief and doctrine.

Today when a person says they "believe," they most often mean they agree to a prescribed doctrine embraced historically by a specific group of Christ followers. That position cheapens the challenge to which Jesus was inviting us. Our response to Jesus' call to believe could be reduced to saying, "I believe He lived and that God exists." *Pisteuo* is more than a simple mantra or a trite set of concepts that wrap a straight jacket around Jesus' intentions in the use of *pisteuo*.

Jesus longs for us to become transformed *pisteuo*/all in people. Don't reduce that powerful action word to a set of doctrines. We are to dedicate every fiber in us to the mission and purpose of going *pisetuo* "all in" and having crucial conversations that will lead others to do the same.

I had to learn how to pronounce it, and now I'm making it my life's mission to learn how to live it. *Pisteuo*, is pronounced "pist-yoo-o." Only when I connect with the heart of the Father do I really begin to understand *pisteuo*. Verbs describe movement, and *pisteuo* points to a changed heart.

Pisteuo is where the follower must find a new capacity to trust, faith to embrace, hope to keep moving forward. It is a gift for difficult days ahead. Jesus tells us *pisteuo* makes us "children of God:"

"For those who pisteuo/believed in his name, he gave the right to become children of God."

- John 1:12

It also is a critical dimension of what un-leashes salvation for a Christ follower:

"Whoever believes/pisteuo and goes all in, and is baptized will be saved, but whoever does not (pisteuo by going all in) will be condemned… "   - Mark 16:16

Everything that Jesus desired for us comes together in that passage. You can hear His heart for us. He was not content for us to simply create a cognitive space in our cranium for the concept of "God." He longs to be connected to us, and to restore us.

Pisteuo has become my focus word. I process my life through the challenge of Christ to be "all in." This word *pisteuo* has so many dimensions. To translate it as "believe" cannot contain the tsunami of love we receive from the Father. The Father went all in when He gave Jesus. That passion continued when Jesus took the greatest risk in human history. This *pisteuo* experiment could have fallen flat. How much more vulnerable could the creator God become than to womb dive into the human experiment?

True *pisteuo* creates a transformed life. You hear the *pisteuo* cry in this statement:

> *"Whoever **pisteuo/believes** in him is not condemned, but whoever does not **pisteuo/believe** stands condemned already because they have not **pisteuo/believed** in the name of God's one and only Son."*   - John 3:18

The single greatest use of our lives would be to discover who Jesus is and then adjust our lives to go "all in." When you allow your life to be divinely interrupted, you will allow the Father to *"change how you think"* and to *"change what you care about"*. Before long these interruptions will become what you live for. That is why Jesus gave us a picture of how our "all in" *pisteuo* life eliminates worry,

> *"But seek first his kingdom and his righteousness, and all these things will be given to you as well. Therefore do not worry..."*   - Matthew 6:33

Why dedicate an entire chapter to one Greek word? I am convinced that our engagement in the mission of Jesus hinges on our proper understanding of what Jesus was trying to communicate through *pisteuo*. We cannot possibly know how to engage in effective spiritual conversations if we do not understand why we should go "all in."

Jesus determined whom to invest in based on the amount of *pisteuo* in a potential disciple. Jesus knew how to measure the level of *pisteuo* in people, in towns and villages, and in situations. If people had no *pisteuo* capacity, Jesus would not invest valuable time and energy there.

Even when Jesus launched His mission with the twelve, it wasn't long before He observed a break down within His selected core group. He regretfully announced in John 6:64:

*" There are some of you who do not 'all in' pisteuo/
trust." For Jesus had known from the beginning which
of them did not 'all in' pisteuo/trust…"*

Jesus is clear. His band could not go forward if
they didn't have sufficient *pisteuo*. The power of *pisteuo* is
a gift the Father gives when we repent and embrace Him.
The word is so significant that there is a term for those
who try "the Jesus way", but later do an about face. The
Bible word for this reversal is the word "apostasy," or ahh-
pisteuo. Ironically, this word literally means to "not
pisteuo." When we aren't "all in" *pisteuo* it is so significant
a new term was coined, ah-*pisteuo* or apostasy takes the
breath away from Christians who understand the stark
warning of the scriptural admonition not to ever be
counted as apostate.

In John 6:36, Jesus said, "You have seen me and
yet do not all in *pisteuo*." When religious leaders resisted
Jesus He soberly pointed out their desperate spiritual
condition by calling them apostate or ah-*pisteuo*. Jesus
points out that many falsely claim to be "all in" but are at
heart deceivers. He said the fruit of being "all in" is self-
evident:

"by their fruit you will recognize them." Matthew 7:20

Lip service does not equal *pisteuo*. Fake *pisteuo*
flies in the face of all that Jesus taught. He warns that the
deceived apostasy group may think they are with me, but:

*"Not everyone who says to me, 'Lord, Lord,' will enter
the kingdom…only the one who does the will of my
Father…"* - Matthew 7:21

Too many church people say they are "believers". They love to study their Bibles, but are unable to have a conversation about who Jesus is in their life. They would say they are believers but they don't really know Him. They don't really love Him. They worship their doctrine and Bibles, while mistakenly think they are worshiping Jesus.

It is my sober assessment that regardless of your claims to be "all in" the real evaluation of your belief is not in the claims you make or the ideas you agree with. It is who you know, more than what you know. Do you know Jesus or do you simply know about Him? I know about Donald Trump, I do not know him.

> Jesus warns, *"Many will say to me on that day, 'Lord, Lord, did we not prophesy in your name and in your name drive out demons and in your name perform many miracles?' Then I will tell them plainly, 'I never knew you…"* - *Matthew 7:22-23*

JESUS SATURATION IS PISTEUO?

When I am saturated with Jesus, I will be able to have crucial conversations about Jesus as someone I know. The Bible experts in Jesus' day completely missed Jesus. They were saturated with Bible information. In fact, one day Jesus pointed out that they had no clue who He was in spite of their great Bible information. In John 5: 39– 40, He said,

> *"You search the Scriptures because you think that in them you have eternal life; and it is they that bear witness about me, yet you refuse to come to me".*

They missed the entire point! Being able to skillfully apply Biblical wisdom to financial planning, relationship building, and every other area of life is important and necessary. Jeff Vanderstelt says, "If we fail to give one another Jesus, we lead one another away from Him. We might grow in Bible knowledge, but not in love for Jesus. We might become the most religious pray-ers of all and yet be talking to the wrong god. We could have our finances in order while our hearts are completely out of order because we are doing it all for the wrong reasons."[10]

If we don't know who Jesus is, it will show up in our conversations. Have you ever been immersed in a country where you did not speak the language but you knew a few words. You probably did your best to communicate. You may have even prepared by taking multiple classes in the language. You possibly received an "A" when you took the language course. It is one thing to know about a language, and an entirely other thing to speak the language.

Have you ever been immersed in a culture that spoke the language you studied in school, you probably found yourself unable to hold much of a conversation. At the end of the day, you probably were exhausted.

When we don't know Jesus, but we try to speak of Him, we will end the experience feeling fatigued. Have you ever tried to share your faith, only to feel like you were trying to communicate in a foreign language

---

[10] Vanderstelt, Jeff, Gospel Fluency: Speaking the Truths of Jesus into the Everyday Stuff of Life (Wheaton, IL: Crossway, 2017), p 30

environment? Too often we learn Christian words, but we can't speak of Jesus. We must know Him to be able to speak of Him. We must become saturated in Him to be able to live at the pisteuo level Jesus desires for us.

Becoming saturated in Jesus means that we will soon be able to speak about how Jesus influences every aspect of life, every situation we face, and every issue we address. We will know when we have had a pisteuo experience with Jesus. We will soon find that we can fluently speak of Him. When we go all in, it is not long before He will impact our thoughts, our finances, our relationships, and we won't be able to stop having crucial conversations.

A pisteuo relationship with Jesus will shape how we handle disappointment, anxiety, and trouble. If we are able to speak about Jesus from a first hand perspective, others will take notice and we will continue to be changed. In Ephesians 4:15, Paul encourages us to be able to speak in every situation about Jesus who hopefully will be the focus of our lives. In other words, if we are going to grow up to be like Christ, we have to grow up saturated with the very life of Jesus coursing through our veins. We will discover that we have naturally engaged in pisteuo.

Pisteuo is the substance, currency, and essence of how we please and connect with the Father Son and Holy Spirit. The writer of Hebrews said:

> "*Without pisteuo/faith* it is *impossible to please God*, anyone who comes to him *must pisteuo/believe…*"
> - Hebrews 11:6

P*isteuo* is the gift we receive from the Father, He gives us the power that opens our eyes to see into a new kingdom.

> *"No one <u>can see</u> the kingdom of God unless they are born again."* - John 3:3

Jesus promised to give us a staggering amount of influence, a power that requires embracing an "all in" *pisteuo* posture. In Acts 1:8 Jesus explains that His followers have an assignment of Kingdom proportion as long as they draw a breath. He said:

> *"All things are possible for the one who pisteuo's /* believes." - Mark 9:23

Jesus applied *pisteuo* to nearly every situation. There is a confidence and hope that comes from the "all in" capacity to keep trusting the Father.

I have been amazed at how living a pisteuo based life gives me insight to see things and situations that I otherwise would never see. Usually, what I see are crucial conversations the Father has ready for me.

THE BRIDGE TO ABAN

 EXAMPLE
Bridge To A Jihadist

One winter evening, I was able to see with kingdom/*pisteuo* eyes. I had been praying for an opportunity to be used by the Father in the life of someone new. That was the night I met Aban, a 24-year-old Muslim man, who stood near a gas station beside the freeway dressed in a thin sports coat at least two sizes too big. A stranger pressed a pittance into his hand, mistaking him for a rookie panhandler.

The temperature was in the mid twenties and a cold wind blew hard against his frail, thin body. I ducked into the warm station to pay for my gas. When I came out he was still there shivering in the cold.

I asked him to join me for a meal. I could use the company and he looked like he could use a meal. We ducked into the restaurant next door. I knew he must have a story, he was not panhandling. He just looked scared and lost.

"Tell me your story," I said. Aban had just hitchhiked 180 miles from Atlanta with nothing but the clothes on his back. He took shelter in the gas station trying to wait out the storm, until the clerk told him to buy something or leave. He had no plan, and no destination. He was just running. I did not know it then but Aban was crossing the bridge all on his own, and was in danger of being blown off into the chasm before he could reach the other side.

I learned Aban was raised in an African tribe that had recently converted to Islam. His family was thrilled that he was accepted into the local Jihad University, where he graduated at the top of his class. His academic excellence at the terrorist university won him an all expenses paid trip to America. The terror cell to which he was assigned in Atlanta was active and on the move.

Little did I know that night that we were beginning a relationship that would last the better part of a year and that he would settle down in Knoxville, TN and be my friend. Let's face it, I was the best option for a runaway Muslim terrorist who was fleeing life as a Jihadist. That night he mostly wanted to stay warm. I paid for a hotel room where he could sleep and take a warm shower.

Over the next several months, we met regularly, I coached him on how to get a job, and I helped him find a roommate. Eventually, his story unfolded further. He told me of a recurring dream that had rocked his world when he was in the terror cell. Several nights in a row he was visited by a "shiny guy" who told him to flee the terror cell. The shiny guy told him several things he must do if he wanted life.

Eventually he believed the shiny guy and decided to run from the only security he had known in this strange land. He told the shiny guy he would run if shiny guy would give him someone to help him. I was that guy, the answer to his innocent, infant like prayer of desperation.

Aban fled with no plan for "next." He hadn't considered that his actions put his family in danger. He was only starting to feel the weight of his actions and realizing he would be on the run for the rest of his life. If the cell ever caught up with him his life would end brutally.

For Aban following the shiny guy was a life or death commitment. I drew the bridge icon and shared how I also once had been on the far side of the chasm. I told him the Heavenly Father built the bridge he was crossing and I assured him he can trust this bridge. I told him it leads to amazing life.

I told Aban my story of how the shiny guy had changed my life, and that He had a name, and His name is Jesus. I told him how Jesus was God in human flesh. He could trust what he had experienced. He was not going crazy or tripping on some bad mushrooms.

I told him that every person can be reached by the Father if they do what he did. He just responded in obedience to what he had been shown. The reason the Father is working in what seems to be this strange way is because we have become so broken and disoriented that we need direction. The shiny guy's job is to lead us to the life the Heavenly Father originally planned for us to live. He had appeared to Aban because Aban had become disoriented and needed help. I had to make the gospel story bite size for him. I told him how Jesus had been killed and came back to life as the shiny guy. I was giving Aban context for why the shiny guy had kept hanging out with him. Believe me, conversations about the shiny guy produced lots of questions from Aban.

Over the next several weeks Aban's heart continued to soften as he walked across the bridge the Father had provided. He was slowly learning to trust Jesus. He was torn because for years he had been immersed in the river of hatred toward followers of the shiny guy. How do you embrace the very people you have dedicated yourself to destroy? He struggled to be discipled by me, an infidel.

I'd never been in crucial conversations with a person who faced such a stark reality. Aban had taken a huge step of faith without realizing it. This life or death choice would forever shape his life. Our conversation moved rapidly forward. I didn't have to create any artificial tensions to move the conversation ahead. The Father had provided all we could stand.

I realized that the typical Christian "sell job" would not work with Aban. I couldn't promise him that everything would be easy for him once he trusted Jesus.

I didn't have to tell him that following Jesus required him to die to his old life. That life was already six feet deep and growing daisies. His choice was to accept a new life in Jesus, or simply live as a fugitive. Either way, he would live on the run. He needed time to process the death of his old life, and then decide if he would continue to walk across the bridge.

BRAIN TWEAK
We Are Like Aban

Ironically, Aban's situation is no different from ours. We are deceived to think that Jesus is one of many options. We don't realize how stark our condition really is.

You've likely heard the common illustration of the different reactions of two frogs placed into kettles of water. One kettle is boiling and the other is room temperature. The frog dropped into boiling water immediately senses the danger and jumps to safety. The frog in the temperate kettle is comfortable, not realizing the water in which he swims is slowly warming by a flame beneath it and he is being boiled to death. His false security leads to his death.

Aban was like so many, unaware of how hot things were getting around him. The shiny guy in his dream was his wake up call, his stimulus to flee across the bridge before it was too late. I invite you to look around and notice those to whom the Father is speaking, who are waking up to their reality of the fire beneath them. The following chapter will help you tell your story better, so when you engage in crucial conversations you will be able to identify and assist those who are ready to cross the bridge to the Father.

Aban's story is a clear reminder that the initial call to Christ is an inevitable call to die. Such a call has been clear since the first disciples laid down their nets and embraced an identity as followers of Jesus. Jesus beckons these men and us to leave behind professions, possessions, dreams, ambitions, family, friends, safety, and security. He bids us to abandon everything. "If anyone is going to follow me, they must deny their life."

One day Aban disappeared and I didn't hear from him for nearly five months. Then he called to assure me he was safe and still on the run. He had been spooked by the terror cell. He was grateful for our time of crucial conversations. He had learned the ways of discipleship and of following Jesus and he was forever changed. He was excited to find other followers of the shiny guy. They seemed to be everywhere he went. Funny how the Holy Spirit makes that happen.

The Father Himself had built a bridge to Aban. The Father is the ultimate bridge builder. That is why the bridge icon is such a powerful tool. I had been able to speak to him about who Jesus was. I could introduce him to my friend. Aban had been conditioned to reject anything that resembled Christianity. He had not been taught to reject Jesus. I introduced him to Jesus, not a religion.

THE FIRST FOLLOWERS
LEARNED TO SPEAK OF JESUS

The first followers of Jesus became saturated in a culture of Jesus. These followers knew what it meant to die to their old lives and to pisteuo the new life. For these followers pisteuo was an all in propositon. Paul was decapitated. Andrew was crucified in Greece. James was beheaded, and John was exiled. Peter was crucified upside down. Yet they bet their lives it was worth the cost. These men found someone to live for who was worth dying for. In Christ, they encountered a love that surpassed comprehension, a satisfaction that superseded circumstances, and a purpose that transcended every other pursuit. They willingly, gladly, and eagerly gave their lives to engage in crucial conversations with those facing a Christ-less eternity.

"Christianity has been reduced to concerts, conferences, and church services."

Somewhere along the way, we lost the urgency to engage in crucial conversations. We have reduced Christianity to concerts, conferences, and church services. We are satisfied instead to follow current church trends, copy pop culture, or hold intellectual discussions of theology. We have minimized Jesus' message and forsaken His approach.

The protection of our reputation is one of the greatest hindrances to advancing crucial conversations. Jimmy Needham has summarized it well in his def-jam poem Nightlights.

"Be Thou Exalted Over My Reputation"

'Cause applause is a poor form of soul medication

And I've tried it for years but my symptoms remain
Still fretting the day that they'll misplace my name
Still selling my soul for American fame

Treating the promotion of Jesus like a well oiled machine

Advancing His kingdom just to snag some acclaim

Now, I'm both comforted and haunted that it isn't just me though

I see a nation of people needing to feed their own egos
Parading status like steeples
Do we not know it's evil to love ourselves
More than both God and His people?

But see, here's where You turn this poem on it's head

'Cause the greatest among us came as servant instead

And You humbled Yourself to the point of Your death
Apparently love for the Father's glory runs red

So friends, will we point to the Son till our own flames grow dim?

Will our bright lights become merely night-lights near Him?

Words echo once, let them echo again
Be Thou exalted over my reputation

Why do we shrink back from sharing the only life giving message that will provide real answers, and real hope? The primary culprit is the protection of our reputation. Why do we so guard our reputation above the cure for the terminal disease that has gripped the world? Friends, we have become so accustomed to protecting our night lights when we have been commissioned to point to the blazing light of the Son.

Crucial conversations are the primary tool you and I have been given in this resistive politically correct age. So lets point to the Son, until our own lights grow dim, in all of His blazing glory. The only way to do so is to allow Him a new place in our otherwise mundane lives. As He creates change in us, let's be faithful to tell our story. The story that has the power to change the world.

Crucial Questions

Crucial questions
God's power to change things

- If you could wave a magic wand and fix any issue in your world, what would you fix first?

- If God had that magic wand what would He fix first?

- Have you ever wondered why God doesn't wave a magic wand and fix your life? Having said that, God has made big changes my life: have you had God make big changes in your life?

Crucial questions
Life's Journey

- What things have benefited you the most so far in your life's journey?

- Do you ever struggle with trying to control things? What kind of things do you think can be controlled in life?

- What's your favorite thing to do?

crucial

CHANGE

HOW WE THINK

conversations

Story of the Samaritan Cynic
John 4:4-15 & 19-23

John 4:4 Now Jesus...had to go through Samaria. So he came to a town in Samaria called Sychar...,Jesus, tired as he was from the journey, sat down by the well. It was about noon. 7 When a Samaritan woman came to draw water, Jesus said to her, "Will you give me a drink?

John 4:9 The Samaritan woman said to him, "You are a Jew and I am a Samaritan woman. How can you ask me for a drink?

John 4:10 Jesus answered her, "If you knew the gift of God and who it is that asks you for a drink, you would have asked him and he would have given you living water.

John 4:11-12 Sir, the woman said, "you have nothing to draw with and the well is deep. Where can you get this living water? Are you greater than our father Jacob, who gave us the well and drank from it himself, as did also his sons and his livestock?

John 4:13-14 Jesus answered, "Everyone who drinks this water will be thirsty again, but whoever drinks the water I give them will never thirst. Indeed, the water I give them will become in them a spring of water welling up to eternal life.

John 4:15 The woman said to him, "Sir, give me this water so that I won't get thirsty and have to keep coming here to draw water.

John 4:6 He told her, "Go, call your husband and come back." "I have no husband," she replied. Jesus said to her, "You are right when you say you have no husband. The fact is, you have had five husbands, and the man you now have is not your husband. What you have just said is quite true.

John 4:19-23 Sir, the woman said, "I can see that you are a prophet"...Jesus said, "a time is coming and has now come when the true worshipers will worship the Father in the Spirit and in truth, for they are the kind of worshipers the Father seeks. 24 God is spirit, and his worshipers must worship in the Spirit and in truth."

"Non-discipleship is the elephant in the church; it is not the many moral failures, financial abuses, or amazing general similarity between Christians and not Christians. These are only the effects of the underlying problem."
- Dallas Willard

"Everyone who drinks this water will be thirsty again, but whoever drinks the water I give them will never thirst... it will become a spring of water welling up to eternal life."
John 4:11-13

CHAPTER 8

CRUCIAL CONVERSATIONS ABOUT NEW LIFE

CONVERSATIONS
With A Samaritan Cynic

The next morning, it was time to begin the return trip home. After the late night encounter with Nicodemus, Jesus and his tribe head north into hostile Samaritan country. It's a hot day and the travel is hard and slow through the coastal hills. Needing some food and a bucket to draw water, the disciples leave Jesus by a local well while they search.

A woman with a bucket approaches the well where Jesus rests. She obviously knows how to dodge the local crowds and is a complete outsider. Most locals would avoid heat of midday to draw their water.

Jesus makes a radical move by initiating a conversation. Notice, He initiated the conversation by asking her a question. She didn't respond to the question. Imagine her shock. A Jewish man would never initiate a conversation with a Samaritan woman. Neither would a Jewish man be vulnerable enough to ask her a question. The Jews and Samaritans were bitter enemies. Centuries before, Babylon had conquered Israel and moved many conquered Jews back to Babylon. Some Jews who were able to hide and stay behind ended up marrying non-Jewish Canaanites and formed a new tribe, the Samaritans. They combined the Jewish and Canaanite religions and created a bastardized syncretistic religion. Jews considered Samaritans inferior in every way. That's the first reason she is surprised Jesus is even speaking to her. On top of that, it was scandalous for a Jewish man to speak to any strange woman in public.

So when Jesus speaks to her, He deliberately reaches across almost every significant cultural barrier. He spans barriers of race, society, gender and morals. A Jewish male should have nothing whatsoever to do with her. But He doesn't care, He reaches out to her to build a bridge.

Do you see how radical that is? He reaches right across all the human divides to connect to her. She is speechless.

The irony is He needs what she has. He has no bucket for water. He tells her, "If you knew who I was, you would ask me for living water; and if you drink that water you will never thirst again."

What on earth is Jesus talking about? He launches a crucial conversation that connects with her pain. The power of the image goes over our heads. We have ready access to drinking water. Having lived in Israel, I know how pivotal water is in the desert hill country. Real thirst and dehydration is devastatingly painful. To taste water after you have been truly thirsty is about the most satisfying experience possible.

Jesus is saying to this woman who has been rejected all of her life, "I've got something for you that will renew you at the deepest level possible." He draws a parallel to spiritual life from the point of physical thirst. Quenching spiritual thirst has a double benefit. It will also produce "eternal life." He's talking about deep soul satisfaction, about incredible contentment that doesn't depend on what is happening outside of us.

BRAIN TWEAK
Search For Meaning

Our search for a satisfying life almost always begins with something outside of us. Whether your heart is set on romantic love, a prosperous career, or a high position, those goals are externally focused. Jesus says there's nothing outside of you that can truly satisfy the thirst deep down inside you.

Jesus is saying, "I can put this life into you. I can give you a level of inner satisfaction that reaches the deepest part of who you are. This life is not based on outward conditions or circumstance." Jesus listened to the Spirit, and knew how to read people.

Something gets in the way of our hearing Jesus. Perhaps it's our spiritual thirst that distracts us. Somehow we remain blind to the very thing we need and long for. As long as you think you have what it takes to satisfy your inner emptiness you will remain unaware of just how profound your need actually is. Our own echo chambers tell us our dissatisfaction comes from failing to meet personal goals. We can live our entire lives without being honest about the depth of our spiritual thirst.

EXAMPLE
Bridge Building:
Have you ever stopped to examine how Jesus built an intentional bridge to the Samaritan woman? He was deliberate and patient. He saw her as a real person with real needs. He knew that before she could deal with her sin issues, she had to admit her need. As we talked in the last chapter the crucial conversation will not advance until the person is open to becoming more self-aware. Jesus treated her with respect and encouragement instead of judgment and distance. He saw no value in rubbing her face in her dysfunction. Instead, He pointed her in the direction that aligned with the purpose for which she had been created. Perhaps He said, "The days ahead don't have to look like the days behind you."

This crucial conversation ignited a spark in her. The text says that once the woman embraced Jesus' insights, she hurried back to the village to tell anyone who would listen. She was compelled to tell everyone how Jesus gave her a new future and a new hope. She responded like most do when they have a real encounter with Jesus. They typically are eager to tell anyone who will listen.

She was so elated that she left her water pot at the well. She abandoned both her pot and rope, which were valuable possessions. This woman – deemed worthless by her culture – had discovered her actual, eternal value.

Beware of Diversions

TOOL BOX
Creating Tension
Did you notice the way Jesus allowed tension to rise in the conversation? As it did, the Samaritan woman tried to get Jesus off track. He's keeping her focused on her need for God. She starts throwing out phantom issues, like worship preferences. She uses a classic diversion to avoid the real crucial

conversation. Jesus knew this was not the burning issue in her life. This was a learned behavior to divert and dodge when the heat gets turned up.

As you engage in crucial conversations you will see behavior defaults like this one. There are still areas of our country where conversations about worship styles and church programs are part of the local culture. In these areas, it is not uncommon to invite a person to come to an event at your church, or to attend a Sunday morning service with you. A Christian often uses this tactic to soft pedal the impact of the invitation, and pave the way for rejection with no ill feelings. I call this, "going church on them."

"Going church" diverts the conversation from crucial to a "church conversation." They are very different. You must keep the conversation focused in a way that leads to substantive matters. Superficial church conversations are as mindless as any other type of shallow conversation.

We find ourselves in an avoidance game when we invite someone to our church. The game goes like this: I extend a church invitation, the other person politely responds, "Yeah, I'll think about that." In most cases, they are not really considering coming. They are engaging you in a game called "frustrate the Christian." From this time on, every time the invitee sees you, they say, "What time does your church start? I'll try to come some time." In some parts of the country this is a learned behavior of our culture.

This diversion takes the focus off of the real issue – which is seldom about which church to attend. In the above story, Jesus went for the heart of the woman. She was an outcast, and had tried some of the classic diversions. Jesus stayed on mission. He asked her hard questions that led to a genuine heart change in the woman. This transformation impacted the entire community.

Perhaps you're uncomfortable thinking up questions to ask. Just do what Jesus did. When he was beside a well, He asked the obvious. He discussed drawing and drinking water. Start with a topic you have in common. Reduce your questions to a more basic level. Don't shrink back from obvious questions. Jesus noted that she came at the hour when an outcast would arrive. She had no children and this gave Him a clue to follow up about her marital situation. These details led to a transformational conversation.

Asking Obvious Questions

 Tool Box
Asking Obvious Questions

Adults tend to avoid asking obvious questions. Children are masters at obvious questions. Somewhere in our socialization process we learned it is impolite to ask obvious questions. We were taught that's rude and makes people uncomfortable. The old adage, "If they want you to know they will tell you," destines conversations to remain superficial. Of course, we must be sensitive and prayerful that the Holy Spirit will prompt us in this area.

Polite conversations tend to lead us to endless, superficial, one dimensional conversations that go nowhere. I don't know about you, but I am exhausted by the daily banter that surrounds me. I am hungry for a meaningful exchange. There obviously are times when simple, polite conversations are necessary. When we can tactfully and skillfully move beyond the mindless drone of our culture and ask powerful, obvious and even personal questions, it almost always leads to richer, more meaningful conversations.

Jesus engaged common people in significant spiritual conversations after first carefully observing and listening. He was skillful at asking the obvious questions, which penetrate to the core issues. When Jesus asked the obvious, He did it in a thoughtful way. We respond in a non-intrusive way when we are led by the Spirit.

Early in the New Testament, we see that all creation has been waiting for the advent of the Messiah. In the opening chapters of Luke, Jesus makes his first pilgrimage to the Holy City of Jerusalem. Mary and Joseph have taken their young son for His first trip to the temple to offer sacrifice. On the return trip they have a "Home Alone" experience when they discover Jesus was left behind. They scurry back to Jerusalem and when they finally find Him, He is "sitting among the teachers."

Jesus asks the obvious question, "Why were you looking for me?" (Luke 2:49)

His question is loaded with significance. Throughout His life, Jesus consistently asked behemoth questions. They all appear on the surface to be obvious, but they have many layers of meaning. At the close of his life He asks a shocking question: "My God, my God, why have you forsaken me?" Volumes have been written about that question.

Even after His death, Jesus keeps asking obvious questions. In the resurrected state He asks two of His disheartened disciples who are walking away from the city several questions. "What are you talking about as you walk along?" They seem shocked and reply, "Do you not know the things that have happened there in the past few days?" Jesus asks an interesting question. "What things?" Jesus obviously knows what has happened, but He wants to engage them in a spiritual conversation. Details are not what matters. He knows them better than anyone. He wants to hear what they think about His crucifixion and resurrection. After this exchange, He almost immediately appears to Peter on the Sea of Galilee. He asks Peter, "Do you truly love me?" Jesus gets to the point with a direct question.

The incarnate Christ asked questions in the common language to speak of heavenly truths. Jesus embraced a communication style that built bridges and opened hearts. We can do the same by learning to translate spiritual truth into the everyday vernacular of the people with whom we converse. We don't do this naturally. We have to cultivate and hone this skill, because we have to unlearn our current approach of church talk. It is amazingly simple to do when we allow the Holy Spirit to lead us.

There is a skill to asking powerful questions. Jesus' questions are typically open-ended rather than closed-ended. A closed-ended question implies a correct answer is needed to fill in the blank. It's often a yes or no. They seldom produce effective spiritual movement.

Asking open-ended questions is harder. We more commonly ask questions to drive the conversation toward the answer we are looking for.

In our family I ask closed ended questions all the time. "Is anybody hungry for Mexican food tonight?" That is a closed-ended question. I want to eat Mexican food. I am driving the conversation in my desired direction. It is almost always met with a groan. My family does not feel like I am including them in the discussion when I ask the question that way.

An open-ended question is, "What dinner choices sound good to you?" An open-ended question does not seek to limit the responses. The answer to an open-ended question is not obvious or implied. The way you word the question affects the outcome.

Jesus asked open-ended questions. I tried to find an example where Jesus asked a closed-ended question. I have yet to find one. Compiled in the appendix is a list of 223 questions Jesus asked in the Gospels. You can see how Jesus used questions to engage people in crucial conversations. I continue to be amazed at the power of these open-ended questions. They have the power to cut into the soul. Below are a few questions Jesus asked from the book of Matthew.

- Matt 5:46 Why are you anxious…?
- Matt 5:47 If you love those who love you, how are you different?
- Matt 6:27 By worrying can you add a single hour to life?
- Matt 6:28 Why are you terrified?
- Matt 8:26 Why do you harbor evil thoughts?
- Matt 9:4 Do you believe I can do this?
- Matt 9:28 What did you go to see?
- Matt 6:27 Can any of you by worrying add to your life?
- Matt 11:8 How can you say good things when you are evil?
- Matt 5:47 If you favor only your brothers, how are you different?
- Matt 12:34 Why did you doubt?

Jesus asked these straightforward questions in the opening days as he worked with His disciples. They are simple, but profound. Jesus asks powerful questions that seem obvious, but are penetrating. It all depended on the context. Most of Jesus' questions are profound and obvious at the same time. For example the last question in the list "Why did you doubt?" is one of His best questions.

If I arrive at an appointment early, my buddy might say, "Wow you made it through the traffic, and you're early." If I replied, "Why did you doubt?" that is not a profound question. Jesus asks a simple question that struck at the heart of the deeper issue. He made the disciples consider their capacity to rely on Jesus in a stressful situation.

In Matthew 14:31, Jesus asks Peter the same question, "Why did you doubt?" The back story is that Peter is learning to trust Jesus. Peter works up the courage to follow Jesus even though everything in him says don't. He timidly steps out of a perfectly good boat into the black, murky torrent of a violent storm. He already was afraid when he was in the boat, now he is attempting to walk on the turbulent water. The experiment in trust was working.

"Hey, I'm walking on the water," he's thinking. Then it hit him. "I just stepped out of a perfectly good boat and I'm walking on WATER!" He realized what was really going on and he froze, and started to sink. In the middle of the sea, he and Jesus talk about it while standing on the water's surface.

Jesus looks him in the eye and asks, "Why did you doubt?" That is a great, but obvious question. Jesus is in effect saying, "Peter, you took the first step, what came over you after you committed to step out of the boat?"

Jesus knew that if he could lead Peter to answer that, the revelation would serve him well in the future. "You are going to face situations just like this," Jesus' question implied. "And I will not be physically there to pull you from the suffocating abyss. Will you still continue to follow me?

Reflect on these 223 questions that Jesus asked (Appendix A). Jesus' skill and wisdom are revealed in them. They were simple and obvious, but profound.

The questions of Jesus are so central to Jesus' ministry. His direct questions are not easy to hear, but they inspire, convict, and challenge at the same time.

Albert Einstein said, "If I had an hour to solve a problem and my life depended on the solution, I would spend the first 55 minutes determining the proper question to ask, for once I know the proper question, I could solve the problem in less than five minutes." [11]

The right question is a gift the Father gives to the right person who will be open to receive the gift. Receiving the right question has a way of changing how we think. It has a way of burrowing deep into our cerebral cortex.

Modern Christians have developed the habit of working to give right answers. Our focus on giving right

[11] Copenhaver, Martin B.. Jesus Is the Question: The 307 Questions Jesus Asked and the 3 He Answered . Abingdon Press.Kindle Locations 1778-1800)

answers will keep us from discerning the right question. If the question is wrong none of our answers work.

Following Jesus is living our lives in response to the questions He asks of us. Our lives will begin to change when we allow the questions of Jesus to puncture our protective veneer.

In the back of the book you will find Appendix "A". This is a more developed list of obvious questions Jesus asks. Let these questions stir you. Our lives won't impact anyone until we allow the questions of Jesus to pervade our experience and our thinking. As I have learned this skill, I have seen it open opportunities that otherwise never would have developed.

CREATING OPPORTUNITY BY ASKING QUESTIONS

I have an unconvinced neighbor. Over the past three years, we have forged a friendship. He is an urban outdoor type. I have taken him on several whitewater kayak trips. As we connect he's become increasingly more open and honest. The first two years, he was not receptive when I gently asked a few obvious questions to determine his spiritual receptivity. He had little interest. I've been praying, "What obvious questions should I ask him?"

Recently, he mentioned a difficult situation with his boss. His boss was acting in a dishonest way, and he didn't know what to do. This conflict allowed me to ask him a series of questions related to how he was handling the pressure. I asked an obvious question and said, "What are your greatest concerns about the situation?" That obvious question opened him up to share some personal details. I told him I would be praying for him tomorrow when he had to confront his boss.

The next day I asked him how it went. He was touched that I had followed up with him. Because I had asked him a series of obvious questions the day before, he felt like he could trust me. He told me he had prayed about the situation. This opened up the opportunity to ask some more obvious questions.

"Is that something you've done much before?" I asked. He said only when things get tough. "I do the God thing when I need help," he confessed, then said, "But it seems different for you."

I took that perfect opportunity to share about how my relationship with Jesus has provided divine council and direction on a daily basis. Then I asked him, "How do you handle stress and problems?"

He said, "I've prayed when I've been in a bind, and I'll go with the family to church for funerals and such, but that's about it for me."

I was listening carefully so I knew what to ask next. "Do you think that has helped?"

He said, "I really don't know, I guess it could. My brother is a big time church guy. I've seen it work for him."

"Do you think it's church that makes the difference for him or something more?" I asked.

He said, "I really don't want to discuss this with him because when I do he gets all amped up and gets to preaching. I just stay clear of that topic with him. We all do.." (as he laughs) Then he said, "This stuff is really important to you, isn't it?"

This is called a defining moment. How you answer this question will either move the conversation forward or things will bog down in the wrong stuff.

So far, he has been slow to respond to any opening I have given him. His distance is a result of his past experiences with other Christians. He probably doesn't want this God thing to ruin our relationship. The last thing he wants to do is to have to start to dodge this topic with me, even though there is a glint of interest on his part.

I briefly shared that it wasn't church that motivated me. It was a personal relationship with Jesus that made all the difference.

"How does that work?" he asked.

So I asked him, "Are you being polite, or do you really want to know?"

"Yeah I'd like to know," he said, "as long as you don't go off on me." (laughs)

I shared a one-minute version of my life change story. I was careful not to dump the full load on him after he had shown a spark of interest. My brief story was enough kindling to feed the fire. That entire exchange only lasted five minutes until he changed the subject. And I let him.

After two years of investment I finally was given the opportunity to share how my life had been changed by the transforming work of Christ. This process can be slow with someone who is far from Christ, or who has been burned by an experience. It takes time to cultivate a tiny spiritual spark. It is essential not to think you have a green light when all you have is a yellow light. As soon as you see a yellow light you must slow down. This man's brother ran through red lights and never knew the damage he was doing. I am sure he has the best intentions, driven by his love and concern for his brother.

The bridge to my neighbor was built when I asked him a couple of simple, obvious questions. We fail to realize the power of a simple, obvious question that is asked in love. The next time you are tempted to filter out the obvious question, try asking the Holy Spirit for direction. Ask Him, "Is this a question that you are feeding me that will open a crucial conversation?" If it is, "How can I 'do so with gentleness and respect?'" (1Peter 3:15).

Crucial Questions

Crucial Questions
For Bridge Building

Crucial Questions
Obvious questions Jesus asks

- Why do you call me "Lord, Lord," and don't do what I say? (Luke 6:46)

- Why do you break the command of God? (Matthew 15:3)

- What were you arguing about? (Mark 9:33)

- Who are the faithful and wise managers? (Luke 12:42)

- Why are you testing me? (Mark 12:15; Matthew 22:18)

> If we are to love our neighbors, before doing anything else we must first see our neighbors…we must see not just their faces but the life behind their faces.
> **-Frederick Buechner**

> If we truly love people, we will desire for them far more than is within our power to give them, and this will lead us to prayer.
> **-Richard Foster**

CHAPTER 9

CRUCIAL CONVERSATIONS, ASKING INNOCENT AWE QUESTIONS

BRAIN TWEAK
Build A Bridge

I don't know exactly when it happens, when we leave the innocent zone of childlike awe. We grow cynical and skeptical as we age and get more "worldly wise." We lose our amazement, curiosity, exploration, fascination, surprise, and astonishment of the magnificent world in which we live. Why would we relegate such wonder to children alone?

Jesus seemed to retain the ability to see the world with awe. That's quite remarkable considering that "The world was made through Him" (John 1:10). That verse also says, "The world did not recognize Him." The world overlooked Him. Who would expect the creator of the world to have a childlike sense of awe toward His creation and an innocent dependence on His Heavenly Father. It was from this vista that Jesus shaped innocent awe questions.

Why is a child able to ask penetrating and thought provoking questions? It's because they haven't grown the social filters of adults. How many times have you been amazed at a child's questions or been impacted by a child's simple insights? There is a reason we say, "out of the mouth of babes." Children can blurt out questions that seem impolite, but often are provocative. We can learn the skill of asking obvious questions with the social and relational skills of an adult.

The institutional church is much more comfortable with Jesus as a provider of answers than an asker of questions. He knew that answering questions does little in the big scheme of things. He would rather be the Savior who engages us in conversation than one who is an incarnate theology textbook. Our lives don't change if we are not in the conversation. One-way communication has little value. Jesus knew that our souls do not hunger for theological answers. They seldom produce life change.

Jesus did not come to inform us. He doesn't offer 10 spiritual tips for better quiet time. He wants to engage us so we will be transformed. He asks the hard questions that create an internal hunger for the Father.

Embracing this type of thinking will take some intentional work. Innocent awe is the springboard that propels us into the world of discovery. We would all but miss the world of awe and wonder if we didn't have children in our adult lives to draw us back. They put vibrant color and adventure into our world. The adult version of the world quickly fills with practical, efficient, grey cities of high function but virtually no innocent awe. The more a culture eliminates God from its core the more it lives in a colorless, tasteless world of systems and predictability.

It's easy to end up "awe-less" in a world that prefers answers over questions and information over exploration. If you are honest, has it been a long time since you've allowed yourself to venture into a place of innocent awe?

The Father has placed us in a world that naturally draws us like a tractor beam toward awe and wonder. But we resist that tug because it's not "cool" to be awestruck. We want to act like we've been there before, seen it all and done most of it.

Look around you. Most people live in an awe starved world. When we don't approach the world with awe-based questions, we tend to miss conversations the Father has waiting for us.

Allow the Father to recreate innocent awe in you. Before long, you'll rediscover an innocent curiosity that will create a hunger to know more about the world that others live in. You will no longer define your world as "Christians and non-Christians."

This polarization did not exist in the New Testament church. This divide prevents us from effectively engaging in life changing spiritual conversations.

As innocents in awe, we give up the deception that we must have all the answers and we can regain a humble heart, like a child. This is the place Jesus desires for you to live. He said, "Whoever humbles himself like a child is the greatest in the Kingdom…" (Matthew 18:4). Jesus indicates we must take hold of the process of humbling ourselves. This critical step allows us to move into spiritual conversations authentically by eliminating canned or awkward transitions.

CONVERSATIONS
Innocent Awe Conversation

The practice of innocent awe will almost magically give you the affable questions that open up powerful spiritual conversations. When people begin asking and seeking, they begin the process that leads them to the Father. Jesus promises us, if we "ask it will be given to you…" (Luke 11: 9). The Father has created each one of us to naturally wonder about things we can't grasp without asking, seeking, and (eventually) knocking on the Father's door for help. This built-in inquisitiveness is just waiting to be unleashed. This same skill that leads us to the Father will open a new world of spiritual conversations.

When we approach people with genuine innocence and awe we are offering to engage with them, and listen to them about what matters most in their life, career, and family. Our questions invite people to search for their own answers and naturally stimulate them toward spiritual exploration.

Innocent awe questions create an atmosphere that the Holy Spirit uses to move and stir one's inner soul, help people discover new things about themselves, and nudge them one step closer toward a new life in Christ.

The average Christian shrinks back from sharing his or her faith because they are afraid they cannot answer faith questions that might come their way. I have news for you: nobody wants to hear those answers. So don't let that fear paralyze you.

I have fallen prey to this mistake, trying to be the answer man. It is far better simply to engage people and listen to their story. When we get a chance to share what Christ has done for us, we should share. From there it is our job to follow the lead of the Holy Spirit.

As long as we keep answering people's questions, we will struggle to identify disciple-able people. We will also miss the opportunity to help them find the answers for themselves. Jesus knew every question has the potential to open up a discipling conversation.

The innocent awe question takes a different approach from "I've got all the Bible answers" style. The next time someone comes to you searching for a quick answer, remember to ask an innocent awe question so you can find the reason behind the question. Fight the temptation to give a quick biblical answer that affirms your great and grand knowledge base. Answers seldom lead to crucial conversations.

HOW DID CHRISTIANITY BECOME INFORMATION BASED?

BRAIN TWEAK
Maturity Isn't Measured
By Knowledge

About 240 years ago, a philosophical movement arose which came to dominate the world of ideas. During this "Age of Enlightenment", philosophers sought to understand everything based solely on reason, with no regard for matters of faith. The Christian church felt it was under assault, with its authority and influence steadily undermined.

AGE OF ENLIGHTENMENT MOVEMENT

This movement started in the universities and rapidly spread. At its heart was the belief that observable facts and human reason must occupy the center of our culture, not faith in God. This ushered in the era of humanism.

The Church could have responded in many ways. It could have discipled Christ followers to live unto God only and reject opposing ideology. It could have resisted this philosophy that undermined the organic movement that Jesus launched. It could have encouraged its scholars to offer a reasoned alternative worldview that points to the hand of God in creation.

Instead, the institutional church collectively embraced the "enlightenment of reason" that saw no need for God. This philosophy said, "We need not look beyond our own intellect. Enlightened individuals will solve any problem. Looking to a mythical God is a waste of time."

This path led to the single greatest destructive impact to Christ's church. For ten generations Christians have been propagating a Christian version of the false teaching of the enlightenment. In a nutshell, the baptized version of enlightenment says we will become mature Christians when we reach a level of biblical illumination. We arrive there after countless hours of study and learning. Spiritual maturity is knowing and learning the right information. This philosophy has produced thousands of Christian schools all over the world, from kindergarten to universities and seminaries. If Jesus believed this kind of enlightened populace makes the best disciples then He would have come to launch the Kingdom of God education system.

This philosophical course has sterilized modern day Christians from having vibrant reproductive conversations. We are too preoccupied with our Bible studies, large group Sunday Bible classes, and taking classes at a local Bible college to engage in crucial conversations. We have promoted biblical literacy at the cost of following Jesus' command to "go… make disciples." That process must start with effective crucial conversations.

As enlightenment culture took root, the church made a shift. It wasn't long until churches that featured great orators were bursting at the seams. Speakers like Charles Spurgeon, John Wesley, and John Calvin packed in thousands of eager learners. Not only did the Church embrace large public gatherings, it began to become divided under the different philosophies that each teacher developed. The primary purpose of those oratorical extravaganzas was to feed the crowds biblical information. It wasn't long until groups identified themselves as Wesleyans, Calvinists, Campbellites and a host of others. The Sunday school became popular during the enlightenment movement. After all, you couldn't be a growing disciple unless you were learning vast amounts of Bible.

The Christian church acquiesced to the new movement and before long it had developed a Christian version of the very philosophy that threatened to undermine it. Its central idea was that knowledge leads all of humanity into a new enlightenment. It is the same strategy the enemy of our soul devised when men attempted to build the tower of Babel to reach heaven, as is told in Genesis 11.

Today, most Christians act as if they believe if we learn enough theology and information, we will become mature, obedient, "enlightened" Christians. The heart of this deception is, "If we learn enough about God we could replace Him with our knowledge of Him."

We have fallen for the core arrogance that assures us we can achieve a mature, enlightened status in the power of the flesh, that by logic and reason we can replace our need for God. The original deception at Babel was, "Come let us build for ourselves…" Genesis 11:4.

This core deception attached itself to the genuinely transformational awakenings during the nineteenth century revival era. It has progressively paved the way for liberalism and neo-classicism. Every election cycle you hear enlightenment propaganda. "Our problems will be solved with better education. More money must be spent on education. That is how we will lift people out of poverty."

The church version of that message is we tell people to accept the right information about Jesus, believe in Him, be baptized, and join a local church, and engage in multiple Bible studies. If we do all of the above with effective sin moderation, then we will be good enough to go to heaven. The enlightenment plan is a perversion of the Gospel. It doesn't produce transformed followers of Jesus. If there is not genuine repentance and the presence of the Holy Spirit in a person's life, there will never be real life change.

The enlightenment movement has sterilized the movement that Jesus launched. It has produced followers with full brains but un-regenerated hearts. We cannot study the Bible enough, nor do enough good things to make us acceptable to the Father. Neither our admission to heaven nor our relationship to the Father can be achieved by anything we do.

Innocent Awe Questions, not information, open hearts

A person with a burning issue may have genuine discipleship momentum. Don't crush their spark by providing an easy answer. Jesus mastered the skill of opening hearts. He seldom provided answers to questions. He specialized in innocent awe questions.

You can't strong arm someone into the kingdom with answers and information. We have discussed how ineffective most of our Christian conversations are when we try to force our agenda instead of zeroing in on topics people want to explore.

THE THREE PARTS OF LIFE ICON

TOOL BOX
Three Parts Of Life

I recently had a spiritual conversation that illustrates how the innocent awe principle works. On my way to an event where I would have an assigned seat, I began to pray for the encounter I knew was coming. I introduced myself and began to get to know those to my left and right. To my left was a 35-year-old man named Todd. We exchanged some basic, superficial, safe information. About 15 minutes into the meal, I saw the opening for an innocent awe question.

"You mentioned your daughter," I said. "Tell me about her. She sounds amazing." (This is an innocent awe question.) His face immediately lit up. We talked for 10 minutes about Carlie. He mentioned that she keeps asking hard questions. I asked, "What kind of questions is she asking?" (another innocent awe question)

He gave a general answer. I asked him what has been her hardest question? This is a play-by-play of that conversation:

Todd: She keeps asking about God.

Me: What do you tell her?

Todd: I don't know what to tell her. My parents didn't answer that question well for me.

Me: Do you remember when you asked them that question?

Todd: (pause) Yeah, I do. I remember thinking there must be a God that created everything.

Dan: So where are you now on that topic?

Todd: In college, I learned God does not exist. I don't know what to tell her.

Me: It sounds like you are struggling with what you learned in college.

Todd: Maybe, I just don't want to take that away from her.

Me: Take what away from her?

Todd: You know, the chance that there maybe is a God.

Me: It sounds like you would like for there to really be an all knowing, all powerful God.

Todd: I can't go there.

Me: Why not?

Todd: I don't know, maybe I would like to believe that. I think I wished my parents would have answered that question for me. Maybe I would have come to a different conclusion.

Me: How would that have changed things?

Todd: I don't know.

Me: You have mentioned that you are finishing an MBA. You've talked about regularly doing cross fit. A few years ago, I read in the Bible, that we are created with three main parts. We have been given a mind, body and soul. I, like you, have spent several years in grad school developing the mind. I also spend a lot of time working out, and developing the body. When I read that verse, I realized that I had not spent much time developing my soul. The Bible teaches that the soul is the eternal part of me that lives forever. I realized that I needed to spend at least as much time exploring that portion of my life as I did the other parts. (As I discussed the three parts I held up three fingers. The pointer finger was the one I referred to as the soul part.)

Todd: I probably have never developed that (soul) part of my life. That probably explains why I can't answer Carlie's question.

Me: I have a copy of a book that has been of help to me. I would love to give you my copy. Would you want to look over it? It is called "The God Questions."

Todd: Yeah I would love to.

Me: I would like to stay in touch with you as you explore this topic.

Todd: Yeah, let me give you my number.

Our new goal should be to identify where the Holy Spirit is already at work. Ecclesiastes 3:11, says that God has "set eternity in the hearts" of all men and women.

That verse tells me that everyone has a hunger and desire to explore the eternity category placed in their hearts.

Todd assumed he didn't have a need for God. His little 9-year-old daughter awakened that in him. A few innocent awe questions transported Todd back to his innocent awe era. This exploration allowed him to reconsider an area of his life that had been temporarily plugged with a hollow answer from a freshman college course he took 16 years earlier.

An innocent awe question picked the lock on his heart. This question opened the possibility of another reality for Todd. The series of innocent awe questions allowed me to avoid a confrontation and paved the way for a heart-to-heart spiritual conversation about the most important topic we could ever discuss. Under the thin veneer over his heart lay a sufficient answer.

Following are four things to look for when stepping into an innocent awe conversation:

- First, be spiritually prepared for the encounter. Praying before the event put me on high alert for a crucial conversation. The nature of the event guaranteed extended conversation with other participants.
- Second, listen carefully to what people are saying. Innocent awe questions will spring to mind if you let them.
- Third, look for questions that can move people to think more deeply about their lives and how the Father might want to move in their life.

•<u>Fourth</u>, the good news is that you don't have to
force God into the picture. He is already there
ahead of you.

Innocent awe questions are intended to help a
person discover his or her need for the Father. He
becomes the obvious answer, so you don't have to sell
Him as the answer. You just have to ask the right
questions to allow others to discover Him themselves.

HOW TO HAVE EFFECTIVE
INNOCENT AWE QUESTIONS

When you are asking innocent awe questions, move
carefully. If you are too forceful, it will feel intrusive.
Remember, you are moving through a person's delicate
belief system. The goal is not to take control of a
conversation because that usually shuts down all forward
movement.

•Innocent awe conversations emerge from a
genuine fascination with the person you have
been led to pray for and get to know.
•Innocent awe conversations must come from an
authentic desire to better understand
someone.
•Innocent awe conversations are not forced. They
will naturally emerge. As soon as we try to
force the conversation to be about Jesus, it
ceases to be a conversation.
•Innocent awe conversations aren't loaded with
assumptions. I am amazed at how often
Christ followers assume that a person is a

transformed person just because they use Christian language. We can't assume a person has been transformed until we hear evidence of genuine life change showing up in their conversations. Avoid such questions as, "Are you a Christian?" "What church do you attend?" "Have you been saved?" Those questions will give a false positive nearly every time. Innocent awe questions ask the person to tell them about their experiences and understanding.

If you're not discerning, innocent awe conversations can leave the person feeling like they have been grilled by the CIA. Strike a balance between listening with wonder and briefly sharing in an honest, transparent way. This will empower the spiritual conversation to develop naturally.

Good conversations only happen when we have prayerfully listened and we do not speak in the language of Zion or Christianese.

The use of Christianese makes people feel like outsiders. This form of insider language assumes our experience is universal – and it's not.

First steps to innocent awe questions:

If you are concerned that developing a genuine interest in the other person feels forced, ask the Father to create a new relational gear in you. The Holy Spirit loves to do this in us. Creating a genuine interest in others is as simple as shifting focus from your world to look at their world. Ask about their children. Ask what motivates them. Ask about their dreams. Just ask and listen for the next question to develop.

Take the time to genuinely think about those the Father places on your mind. I have discovered that when someone comes to mind it is often a work of the Spirit. This prompting may be the result of them crying out in prayer, and the Spirit is prompting you as an answer to their prayer. It may be that a set of circumstances has emerged and this newfound tension has produced a new level of spiritual receptivity. A host of other spiritual elements may be taking place that you cannot see at this time. Whatever the case, learning to listen to the promptings of the Spirit is essential for us to engage in effective spiritual conversations.

Be careful not to apply an aggressive apologetic approach. You can't fake innocent awe. It must be genuine. There is no preset script you can learn. The conversation must inform and provide your response. Spiritual conversation from days gone by usually includes a pre-set of approved questions designed to lead a person toward a decision. Often an argumentative apologetic ensues. Most of the cults that come to your door use this method.

You must establish the skill of intently listening. Learn to ask good follow-up questions. If the other person states a strong opinion, you might say, "That's an interesting perspective. I would love to hear how that came together for you."

I can't give you a pre-formed list of questions. At the end of each chapter you will find questions to prompt you to cultivate good questions. They are not to be memorized, but are included to help you learn to form better innocent awe questions.

Have you been in a tense conversation when you couldn't think of what to say? A fall back response can be, "Something you said really stuck with me. I can't get it out of my head. I would love to know more about…" Or "I'm still curious about…."

Innocent awe can be expressed in many ways. Leading with the phrase, "I would love to know more about…" or "I'm curious about…" or "Tell me more about…" are ways to engage in an innocent awe conversation. You'll soon develop skills that soften the questions, and the sense of awe will emerge as you practice. Remember to proceed cautiously and prayerfully. We can't know in advance what another person needs or wants.

It was important to Jesus to hear what was on the hearts of those with whom He talked. He needed to know their level of engagement, so He became a master at making the right questions before teaching a gospel truth. Maybe we should, too.

Crucial Questions
INNOCENT AWE QUESTIONS

Crucial Questions
Innocent Awe Questions

- What are some of your life goals?

- What did you want to be when you were elementary age?

- What dreams have you let go of?

- What dreams are you still hanging on to?

- Are you optimistic or pessimistic about the future of our world?

- Do you think it's easier or harder to raise kids in today's world than it was when you were growing up? What concerns you most when you think about your future?

- What is your dream job? Are you working toward it already?

crucial

CHANGE

HOW WE
APPROACH
PEOPLE

conversations

SECTION 5

Jesus' Conversation With a Man by the Pool
John 5:1-12

John 5:1 Some time later, Jesus went up to Jerusalem for one of the Jewish festivals. Now there is in Jerusalem near the Sheep Gate a pool, which in Aramaic is called Bethesda and which is surrounded by five covered colonnades.

John 5:3 Here a great number of disabled people used to lie: the blind, the lame, the paralyzed. One who was there had been an invalid for thirty-eight years.

John 5:6 When Jesus saw him lying there and learned that he had been in this condition for a long time....

John 5:6 Jesus asked him, "Do you want to get well?

John 5:6-7 Sir," the invalid replied, "I have no one to help me into the pool when the water is stirred. While I am trying to get in, someone else goes down ahead of me.

John 5:8 Then Jesus said to him, "Get up! Pick up your mat and walk.

John 5:9 At once the man was cured; he picked up his mat and walked. The day on which this took place was a Sabbath...

John 5:10 and so the Jewish leaders said to the man who had been healed, "It is the Sabbath; the law forbids you to carry your mat.

John 5:11 But he replied, "The man who made me well said to me, Pick up your mat and walk."

John 5:12 So they asked him, "Who is this fellow who told you to pick it up and walk?"The man who was healed had no idea who it was...

Change comes from small acts that move us, not from
grand pronouncements.
-Seth Godin

Then Jesus said to him, "Get up! Pick up your mat and walk."
John 5:8

CHAPTER 10

CRUCIAL CONVERSATIONS WITH A DOWN AND OUTER

CONVERSATIONS
Healing At The Pool

In our last vignette, Jesus encounters the woman by the well. She created quite a stir as she encouraged the townspeople to follow Jesus. After the Samaritan encounter, Jesus and the group walked 20 miles north to their home by the sea. For several days Jesus trained his 12 disciples but before long it was time for them to trek south to Jerusalem. The writer opens the next scene with Jesus and his select band of misfits entering Jerusalem. Like most visitors to Jerusalem who come for high holy days they go straight to the Temple to take care of religious business. The scene opens with Jesus and company standing beside a pool of murky water that flanks the Temple. Contaminants float in the water, the debris provides evidence that the massive crowd has walked through the pool out of religious obligation. They do this to be ceremonially cleansed and qualified to offer sacrifice at the temple. This practice of religious purification is called baptism. Every trip to the temple requires baptism for any devout Jew who wishes to be obedient,

Christians trust the redemptive work of Jesus as complete and feel no need to repeat a religious purification process. Jesus took care of this once and for all.

The camera zooms in on Jesus by the pool with His disciples, perhaps teaching a lesson about the practice of baptism in his new kingdom.

Jesus recognizes a man he has seen laying by the pool since Jesus' earliest trips to the Temple as a child. Jesus engages the man, probably saying something like, "You have been here in this same spot for as long as I can remember. Tell me your story." That Jesus takes the time to ask the man his story is quite remarkable. Pilgrims going through the ceremonial bath would drop coins in the cups of the faceless beggars who line the pathway to the temple. Pilgrims were especially generous because they want to impress God. The tangle of beggars with their deformed limbs, scarred bodies, and distant stares take advantage of that desire.

Jesus cuts to the chase. He asks the beggar with a cup outstretched why he has been in this line for so many years. Jesus leans in and softly asks, "Do you want to get well?" The question implies, "Tell me what is really on your heart. Is this just a panhandling scam, or do you hold a glimmer of hope to become whole?"

If there is no hope in the man's heart then anything Jesus would do or say will be of no value. However, if a spark lurks, this man's spiritual fire could be fanned into flame.

Jesus makes it clear He will not invest time in anyone who doesn't have a glint of *pisteuo*. The man gives a good answer. He has set up camp at poolside for 38 years because he believes people have found healing there. Apparently, as pilgrims have passed through the baptismal waters over the years, some have departed the pool physically healed and restored. He has had the *pisteuo* to sit there and look and wait for some indication that it is his time to hit the water when spiritual lightning strikes. But he's too slow. Maybe his disability is too severe. Someone else plunges in ahead of him and evidently absorbs the healing power.

Jesus is moved by this man's *pisteuo*. The man is misinformed about how healing works, but Jesus doesn't let that distract Him. Jesus is focused on the big picture. He is redeeming broken people, not arguing about theological trivia. Jesus suggests that the man just bypass his pool diving plan and get on with the thing that is really on his heart.

"Buddy, you need to become whole," Jesus might be saying in today's vernacular. "So collect your mat and let's cause a real stir by having you walk out of this place as a transformed follower."

That's all it took,. The man had the necessary *pisteuo* to be healed. As the newly restored man walked from the crowded pool area, mall cops stopped him. They interrogated him about carrying a mat on the Sabbath. Such an action was "work" as defined by Jewish rules, and work is prohibited on the Sabbath. He told them his story just like the blind man: "All I can tell you is that I had the *pisteuo*, and Jesus healed me." The lame man, like the blind man, had several opportunities to tell his story.

 BRAIN TWEAK Remember how Jesus began this
Spirit led Questions encounter? He asked an innocent awe question, like, "Tell me your story." Jesus didn't assume He knew the reason the man had lain so long by the pool. Jesus

asked a heart related question. "What is really driving you?" The man's answer set the course for what happened next. Jesus did not have time to let Himself be distracted by a conman panhandler. Yet He took the time to ask a couple of revealing questions, questions that would help determine if the man is discipleable? Developing the skill to ask innocent awe questions will open up a new world of conversations.

CONVERSATIONS CAN HELP YOU FIND DISCIPLE-ABLE PEOPLE TO INVEST IN

If I ever wanted to drive out of the border city of San Diego in southern California, I had to pass through a check point. Exit points from every direction had expanded lanes with armed agents who checked every car. The guards were trained to make a decision with a glance. They had honed their skills to the point they could absorb an amazing amount of information by asking one or two questions. Their training allowed them to determine whether they would invest more time with you or just let you proceed.

In a similar way, we are looking for those the Spirit is working in and on. We can learn the skills Jesus possessed. We can follow the Spirit's lead to quickly assess the receptivity of those we're led to connect with. The basics can be taught, but the skill is really developed through practice. Crucial conversations are nothing more than learning how to partner with the Holy Spirit to find the people He wants you to invest in and lead through the discipleship process.

THE RIGHT QUESTIONS
CAN HELP YOU CONNECT

In our post-modern world, Christians need to master the skill of asking questions to remove barriers. Jesus was the master at forming a question that measures a person's spiritual receptivity. The right question can help others solidify their beliefs and create a hunger to learn more about Jesus.

As Christ followers, our belief system and worldview goes against virtually everything our culture holds dear. Consequently, it is important that we know what questions to ask, so we can quickly identify a point to build a relationship. Don't assume that you know how to connect with someone. We all need to do some investigative work to know how to build a relational bridge. When we ask questions, we become so much more relevant.

Christian Bible colleges and seminaries invest a great deal of resources in the area of apologetics. This course of study is designed to arm Christ followers with tools to win arguments, and defend the Christian faith. This area of study provides great personal value for the student, however it is not very effective for direct evangelism. These days, very few people who are far from Christ will tolerate a confrontational evangelism style. The value of apologetics comes when a Christ follower gains the confidence to engage in meaningful conversations with persons who hold conflicting views. Apologetics was never meant to be the primary bridge for Christ followers to connect to a person far from Christ. You never see Jesus using an apologetic style with outsiders.

Our culture continues to be more and more relativistic. As a result, Christians who are armed with airtight arguments for the Christian faith find their solid logic meets strong hostilities and resistance. Our "tolerance culture" causes nonbelievers to fight back. We are told by the secular world that a Christian position is hateful and filled with micro-aggressions.

We must learn to engage a secular culture differently. When we ask questions in a caring way, our dialogue will be constructive. We need to learn to ask persons questions in a way that exposes their spiritual uncertainty, while lowering their defenses. This approach can create a curiosity that makes them want to hear more.

Conversational signals

Jesus' disciples used a conversational style quite different from that used by most modern Christians. They did not use a disapproving or "parental" tone to "preach at" people, thinking they were communicating with them. This approach is offensive to most in our culture. It has an excessive focus on providing correct biblical information. People will not embrace the life-changing message of the gospel if they don't discover it for themselves. We have moved past a time when an authoritarian lecture would land well with an audience. Today little of our message will be embraced without a two-way exchange.

The Soviet psychologist, and founder of a theory of human cultural and bio-social development, Lev Vygotsky, has said two-way, oral language is the primary way humans process ideas. We have embraced a one way style of communicating for so long that we have to learn new habits. Vygotsky would say that we haven't understood a concept until we can wrap the idea into language and speak about it. Simple exposure to an idea doesn't mean we understand the concept. One-way communication is no longer an effective gateway for learning. Real learning requires dialog.

TOOL BOX
Relational Signals

There are a couple of things to keep in mind as you learn to ask effective spiritual questions. You need to learn to read the relational traffic signal. Everyone you talk to will subconsciously indicate how you should proceed with them.

GREEN LIGHT:
If a person eagerly engages when you ask a question you have a green light. You know that you have hit a point of receptivity and openness.

YELLOW LIGHT:
Sometimes my first question is well received, but my interest becomes too intense. The light will change from green to yellow. Be aware when the spiritual receptivity is waning.

RED LIGHT:
There are times when our questions meet low receptivity. I have been guilty of being quick to speak and slow to listen (James 1:19 tells us to do the opposite). That is usually when I find that I miss important spiritual conversation signals and it does not go well.

Most of the times we run red lights, we do so unknowingly. But a clue is that when we spout opinions we usually come off as condescending. Big red light.

When you cultivate spiritual conversations apply the softer, more personal type of communication that Jesus used. Jesus had a way of sharing information that was content appropriate and would connect with the perspective of the potential disciple. He mastered the skill of asking the right question. His questions always had profound implications.

ICON MT. GOOD PERSON

ICON TOOL BOX
Climbing Mt.Good Person

Everyone has a built in need for God, even if many are not yet aware of their own need. Some crucial conversations will reveal that a person believes he has no need for God. To tell your story using this Icon, the person you are sharing it with will need some agreement that there is a morally good God. When I run into this type of person, I use the Mt. Good Person Icon.

This icon is a tool to adjust the conversation away from their misconception that, "They are good people, and good people go to heaven". This icon may allow you to discuss everyone's universal need for God. If they can admit that they have a need for God, you have opened up the ultimate crucial conversation. The first step toward disciple-ability is when a person can admit that their sin is a condition that has separated them from the Father.

As I draw this, I tell them to think of the mountain peak as perfection. You can ask them if they would agree that only God gets to sit at the top of the mountain, He is the only one who is holy and perfect.

Of course, the dregs of humanity are at the bottom of the mountain. The rest of humanity is somewhere between the foot and the peak. If they agree that there is a morally good God, most will agree with this assessment. When you draw this icon ask them to put a mark somewhere on the mountain that represents

Mt. Good Person

God — Perfection
Jesus Closed the Gap
MLK
Billy G
M3
Bad People
Murders Evil Folks

where they believe they are, based on the life that they have lived so far.

However before I give them the pen, I provide some perspective by saying, "Billy Graham says he is a sinner and is at best mid-mountain. Martin Luther King was a great leader but also had a sinful past. Both men say that being Christ followers helped them to see that they fall way short of the mountain peak of God's perfection. As far as I'm concerned, I am way below those two guys on Mt. Good Person. I have never been falsely thrown in prison, or been beaten for my beliefs. I would say that I am above the bad people category. I place my name in the lower third of the mountain."

With those names on the mountain I hand over the pen. Then I ask, "Where do you think you would be on your climb to being a good person?" Inevitably, the person will place his or her name below MLK. They often respond similarly to the way they do in the conception/birth icon. Most of the time they write their name near mine. They size themselves to be more in my league than in Billy Graham's or Martin Luther King's.

"Okay," I say. "What is your plan to make up your gap? Martin Luther King and Billy Graham had a plan for their morality gap. Jesus offers to take us up the mountain when we can't go it on our own. He said he would make up the distance for us. Martin Luther King and Billy trusted in the same plan for closing the gap between their level of morality and God's standard of perfection.

"That plan is the work of Jesus on the cross. So what is your plan? If you believe that you can rise to the standard of God's holiness on a self-improvement program, you will waste the rest of your life on a moral tread mill. There is freedom when you stop trying to scale the glaciers you cannot climb and choose, instead, to accept the work that

Jesus did on the cross. You can be forgiven. You can live a transformed life. Your goodness altitude can be made up once and for all by trusting in Christ."[12]

This icon serves a different purpose from the conception/birth icon. Use this icon to help a person realize their sinful condition. Often this person is not a cultural Christian, but one who claims to be a "good person who is going to Heaven" based on their goodness. The conception/birth icon is used to assist a person who places their confidence in their cultural Christian activities.

Don't fear their questions

This illustration can stimulate a series of questions that many Christ followers shrink from in fear. You know, questions that non-believers ask don't vary much. You'll often here:

- How could a good God allow evil or hell?
- How can a good God allow suffering?
- Aren't people basically good but need better education?
- If all truth is relative, how does an all powerful God fit into our world?

These are the questions of our day. Down the road, it would be good to know how to respond. Don't think you must have all the answers before you attempt a crucial conversation. If you wait until you can field these questions you will miss real opportunities to grow as a Christ follower.

Develop the skills to ask questions that get to the core of their beliefs. It is surprising how few basic answers there are to life's ultimate questions. Listen carefully and sympathetically as they articulate their beliefs. The details of

---

[12] Hybels, Bill, Just Walk Across the Room: Simple Steps Pointing People to Faith (Grand Rapids:Zondervan) 2006 p 138

systems may differ, but most ideas can be put into a few slots. Here are some examples:

1. QUESTION OF GOD

Determine if a person is beginning from the position that there is no God. Or do they believe in a deistic creator God? If so, ask innocent awe questions that help them to better pinpoint the kind of God they believe in. Most people don't know. They probably have never thought about the question. Is their God relatable or impersonal, finite or infinite, involved in an intimate way or aloof?

When a person comes from a New Age context their god will resemble more of an iconic Star Wars impersonal force than in the God of the Bible. This approach most often comes from a misunderstanding of the God of scripture. Either way, if the person will engage in honest dialog related to how they think it will produce a crucial conversation. For example, if they hold that random selection is responsible for the created world, it would be a waste of time to discuss any biblical account that included miracles.

We could ask questions around how they reconcile the existence of truth. If they believe there is no standard for truth the conversation will go nowhere. Innocent awe questions can explore how they are able to live consistently with such conflict. Remember to let the Spirit lead you to ask questions that will move the process forward.

2. QUESTION OF MORALITY

Why would we choose to act morally if there is no God? A godless reality would declare there is no governing standard for determining right and wrong. Without God, wouldn't we lose all motivation for choosing to act morally?

I know many people who have concluded there is no standard of morality and absolute right and wrong, and yet they are some of the most moral people I know. They advocate "tolerance" in all matters. If there is no standard why do most insist that we should abide by a set of morals when it comes to opposing racism, brutality toward animals, sexual tolerance and a plethora of other cultural hot button topics. Pose an innocent awe question like, "How do you determine what is right and wrong?" Or, "Why do all nations seem to agree on the basic standards of morality?" These innocent awe questions can break open a crucial conversation.

Most atheists don't realize it, but they have adopted a set of guiding morals. However, their worldview doesn't allow them to acknowledge their moral code.

If there is no divine moral standard, then nothing is off limits, including child molestation, and murder. The atheists I know don't want to give up the right to protect their child from monsters who want to do them harm.

The existence of a moral law-giver creates a major problem for an honest atheist. It is incongruent to have it both ways. This line of innocent questions can help to expose a set of beliefs that probably came as a plug and play world view from back in college days.

When we ask good questions, we earn their trust to innocently press into their worldview. This line of questions can expose a person who has not personalized their belief system. A belief system that still has the cellophane wrapper is a belief system that is easy to unravel with a few good questions. An aloof system of untested theory is a system fraught with inconsistencies and incongruent ideas.

The world becomes grey and lifeless if there is no moral standard. Our sense of wonder and beauty come from a creator God who personifies these qualities. This is a form of worship.

The Christian worldview gives us a viable place to ask good questions. This approach places the tension on the person we are talking to – not on us. We need not be controlled by the fear we have to defend our position. It is far better to ask questions that expose their faulty worldview. When most people find their own answers inadequate, they become open to hear, like Peter says, "The reason for the hope that you have" (1 Peter 3:15).

3. Question of self

Everywhere we look our secular world has replaced worship of God for worship of self. There has emerged a new category of questions. Our culture is asking crucial questions related to human sexuality like never before. Our hope is that if those far from Christ engage in a crucial conversation in which a Christian is asking them good questions they will become open to searching and exploring the biblical view of reality.

They may come to understand why there is a hole in their inner life that only Christ can fill. Our culture promises fulfillment when you embrace all things temporal. We have been wired to remain spiritually empty without Christ, even when we grasp for all the material world offers.

The question begs to be asked, "Why does our culture still lack contentment and joy when we have not denied ourselves any pleasure?" While the culture pursues maximum pleasure the pursuit leaves us empty and crying for more of something we can't even name. Christians know the missing piece is found in the transforming work of Christ in their life.

Even a life long hedonist will at some point turn his thoughts to deeper matters. Romans 1:19-21 says they have been exposed to the existence of God, and have no excuse. At some point, everyone has considered that the created order has an origin. Sooner or later a series of God thoughts will pass between their ears. They may repress and resist them, but those thoughts will happen. When they do I want Christians to be there to engage them in a crucial conversation. We can only do this if we are in close relational proximity to them.

Your well-timed conversation can challenge them to quit dodging reality and live as they were designed to live, as children of the Most High God.

A NEW WORLD OPENED UP

Example Bridge Building: I had just moved out of my parents' home to live on my own as a young adult. I had no plans to become a sold out Christ-follower, but in that first year of adulthood, my life completely changed. I had always thought it was my job to climb Mt. Good Person. As a child, I was convinced that God was measuring my moral behavior. He was, "making a list and checking it twice." I was confident that I had earned enough moral merit badges to that point in my life. I headed out to college and before long, everything changed for me. I embraced an entirely new way of living and thinking. The world of following Jesus was new, fresh and exciting. I felt like I had discovered some kind of secret. I knew about churches, I just didn't know they went beyond Sunday morning. I discovered a new community of sold-out Christ followers. This new community became my tribe. Their entire culture focused on following Jesus. I immediately began to tell people about this secret community I had missed for too long, and I didn't want them to miss it too.

Before long I realized there was a huge number of people who said they were Christians, but were not really changed by Christ. This church crowd seemed to be inoculated with just enough Jesus to have an idea of how the transformed Christian life worked, but somehow they were never infected.

I began to investigate this group of Christ claimers who attended churches. In almost every situation they told me they said a magic prayer which meant they would go to heaven when they die. For the rest of their lives they were sentenced to go to church and be a part of the machine that helps others get their "heavenly timeshare deal."

They seemed like salespeople with a high pressure pitch that threatened hell if you didn't buy in. Once you commit to the deal you had to earn points by being good and going to church. But hey, when you die you redeem your points and learn how big of a luxury estate you secured in eternity. This was foreign to the experience and community I had embraced.

Everyone who bought "heavenly time shares" was expected to try to sell as many of these deals as they could to sweeten their own deal – like a multi-level marketing approach. Somehow everyone was earning points.

This all seemed foreign to me. I was already reading the New Testament. My experience was not motivated by a point system. I was motivated by this person I had come to know named Jesus. I was learning to live a life controlled by the Spirit. It seemed odd to present the good news offer of a transformed life as a "heavenly time share."

The striking thing was how little joy seemed to flow from those who were selling the deal. It seemed they were not personally motivated about the very thing they were promoting. Something was missing in their presentation.

Even in those early days I knew the goal should not be to "get someone to say the magic prayer." It should be to take a step toward becoming an "all in disciple of Jesus." Any gospel reading reveals that was obviously what Jesus longs for.

From the earliest days of my spiritual journey I knew the reason that I draw breath is because I have been put here on mission. That mission is to do what Jesus said to do in Matthew 29:19. "As I go," my mission is clear, I am to make disciples. That always begins with a spiritual conversation. If I do that, I will know when I finish the race that I have fulfilled the purpose for which I was created.

Crucial Questions

Crucial Questions
OPENING QUESTIONS

• What prompted you to pursue your career?

• What do you like most about what you do? Least?

• Do you see this as a long-term career, or a stepping stone to something else?

Crucial Questions
LIFE BASED QUESTIONS

• Tell me about your greatest success along the way.

• What's the biggest thing that you've learned so far in your journey?

• What's the greatest advice or piece of wisdom ever passed on to you?

Crucial questions
God's power to change us

• God has made big changes in my life: have you ever let him change yours?

• What things have benefited you the most so far in your life's journey?

• Do you ever struggle with trying to control things? What kind of things do you think can be controlled in life?

"Our most serious failure today is the inability to provide effective practical guidance as to how to live the life of Jesus."
-Dallas Willard

"Too many Christians have accepted Jesus into their hearts… but are not followers of Jesus."
-Mike Breen

CHAPTER 11

CRUCIAL CONVERSATIONS NOT EVANGELISTIC PRESENTATIONS

The mission of the mythological character Sisyphus was to roll a boulder up a mountain only to have it roll back to the staring point – forever. He never could get the satisfaction of completing his mission. There is something inside us that drives us to cross a finish line, to finish a task, to achieve the joy of a job completed. This is why I enjoy the mundane task of mowing my yard. I can stand back and survey a nicely manicured yard. I can cross the finish line of a task accomplished with an hour of effort. Few things in my life can be wrapped up so easily, with such obvious effect.

When we work with other humans, there is no neat, clean line to cross. Humans are messy. We rarely feel like we accomplish much when we are coaching or discipling others. People have no finish lines.

Our Christian culture, on the other hand, has created a fictitious finish line when it comes to faith development. We've made the practice of leading someone to say a "sinner's prayer" a type of finish line. When the prayer is said we declare the one who prayed has crossed the line, checked the box required to be called a Christian, and has punched his ticket to Heaven. This announcement can provide a false sense of security that we never see Jesus offering.

It is natural to want to reduce the important process of moving toward faith to a clean, clear finish line. This formulaic prayer and mysterious finish line has seen some good results in the past. Many have prayed the prayer and lived abundant Christian lives. The problem is as the focus shifts away from discipling people to simply getting them to repeat a prayer and then serve in the local church, we establish a false finish line. We're guilty of spiritual malpractice.

When a person steps across the threshold of faith to trust Christ, that step is only the starting point, not the finish line. If they have truly responded in repentance and have embraced the work of the Holy Spirit in a personal way then they are beginning an amazing journey that will result in discipleship reproduction.

New Testament disciples never embraced the "finish line faith" practice. It emerged over the past couple hundred years. People have been following Christ for centuries without being led in the mystical, revivalistic prayer.

But, aren't we supposed to get those who are far from Christ to cross the finish line and be saved? Close the deal, and check the box? Some even say we're obligated to extend an invitation to pray the "sinner's prayer" at every church event. I am never opposed to giving people the chance to respond to Christ. All I am saying is that it's a tragic mistake to view the first step as the finish line.

I am grateful for Christ followers and churches who want to lead others to become "all in" Christ followers. We just need to look to Jesus for our model more than we do to frontier revivalism.

The practice of leading a person to pray "the sinner's prayer" emerged from the American frontier revivalistic era that produced the Second Great Awakening. It has been an efficient way to help someone take the necessary faith step and follow Jesus.

We can be guilty of rushing the process because we so want to help the person form the words. But this practice produces high pressure and overly focuses the threat of Hell. Jesus clearly taught that there is a real eternal separation from the Father in a place called Hell. He didn't allow the reality of Hell to become a distraction to the advance of the Kingdom of God, or the transformational work of the Holy Spirit.

The "repeat after me" prayer came from a desire to help people move toward a decisive moment. You probably struggled with this decision, and are glad that you chose to step across the starting line of faith. It is natural to want to help others take the faith leap and trust Jesus.

It is far better to engage a person in a conversation about responding to Christ, than to trust in a mechanical formula. It is crucial that a new follower learn to shape their relationship with the Father on their own. We are there to guide them, but not be overly intrusive. When a person shapes their response to Christ in their own words through a prayer of repentance, something powerful happens.

The next step in most churches is baptism. Too many churches make this the finish line. The new believer is abandoned to find his own way. This would be like laying your newborn baby down in it's room and assuming it will know how to navigate from there. You could say the baby has all it needs to survive. It has a climate controlled room, plenty of food in the fridge, and the bathroom is down the hall. One day soon the baby will assimilate into your home. It won't be long until it can open the fridge, and use the bathroom.

Those first steps are critical for the baby to survive. You would never assume it will automatically find its way on its own. It is just as important that a new Christ follower be coached in the ways of following Jesus and be taught how also to help many other disciples.

You have invested a great deal of time and effort in this new Christ follower. You befriended her, invested in her, coached her and encouraged her toward faith. She responded to the offer of Christ. Don't drop her off at the nursery now.

It would be tragic to abandon her at the starting line of the sinner's prayer. Imagine her standing there, wondering, "What just happened?" That's not how you treat a new baby in the family of God.

She would soon realize she was a "prize" and her new Christian family members have moved on to the next evangelism candidate.

WHAT IS THE BIBLICAL BASIS FOR THE FINISH LINE?

A new convert asked me how the magic prayer works. He had been told to just repeat the magic prayer and he would "go to Heaven." He didn't know the biblical basis of the practice is found in Romans 10:9:

> *"If you declare with your mouth, 'Jesus is Lord,' and believe in your heart that God raised him from the dead, you will be saved. For it is with your heart that you believe and are justified, and it is with your mouth that you profess your faith and are saved."*

They had no idea the "want to go to Heaven" prayer was a formula. They were being pressured to do something that should have come in the natural process of repentance. We are tempted to wrap the process into a neat package and slap a bow on it. Our version of the "repeat after me" prayer fits our need to make the process quick, simple and definitive. Too often it occurs in a single encounter.

It's easier to lead a person to a single action and move on than it is to walk with that person through a season of spiritual searching.

In the New Testament, we don't see any examples of Christ followers doing the high pressure spiritual close. In fact, the opposite is true. Jesus allowed people to follow him without pressure to make a formal commitment. Spending time with Jesus would prompt a person either to grow in his faith or self-select out. If the disciple continued to follow he or she would take faith steps. If not, they were allowed to opt out without judgment and condemnation. There was a sense that the Holy Spirit would continue to be at work in their lives.

Jesus explains that if people casually confess "with their mouth," they can be deceived that they are doing something spiritual, but nothing is transpiring. He reminds us in Matthew 7:21-24:

> *"Not everyone who says to me, 'Lord, Lord,' will enter the kingdom of heaven, but only the one who does the will of my Father who is in heaven. Many will say to me on that day, 'Lord, Lord, did we not prophesy in your name and in your name drive out demons and in your name perform many miracles?' Then I will tell them*

plainly, 'I never knew you. Away from me, you evildoers!'"

The problem with most of our "heavenly time share" presentations is we try to make them one size fits all. Real life never works out in neat clean predictable ways. That's why many well-meaning Christ followers, responding to pent up evangelistic guilt, return home discouraged from empty attempts to share their faith.

We should simply find the people the Father has led us to and engage them in crucial conversations to determine how disciple-able they are. There are many benefits to crucial conversations. One of the primary benefits is that they help to identify the people the Holy Spirit is working in and on around you. Once we identify such a person, we need to take a next step with them.

As we walk with them through their spiritual investigation, we will have opportunity to engage in a crucial conversation about surrender, repentance, and salvation.

This person may be an agnostic who is far from Christ or an insider who has considered himself a committed "church person." It is tragically true that a person could be fully engaged in a church and never know the life that awaits them just across the starting line of faith.

Jesus commissioned us to go and make disciples. Finding a disciple-able person was the first step for Jesus. If that was a first step for Him, it should be a first step for us. The following icon can help to explain how to take a trust step to follow Jesus and become a "child of God."

Pisteuo stool icon

Tool Box
Draw the Stool Icon

This icon begins with a simple sketch of a stool with three legs. Describe the three legs as the three points in the passage of John 1:12 – receive, believe, become. Like all the icons, this is a tool to share a spiritual truth best told through your story. Don't just transfer biblical information, but rather share how you took the step to receive Jesus as your Savior.

Practice sharing the steps in your spiritual progression. This icon is a simple way to help your friend move toward releasing his or her old worldview and turning to Christ to save them.

John breaks it down into three simple steps. As you tell your story, draw each leg of the stool. Start with how you came to place your trust in Jesus. Next, tell about how your spiritual confidence and trust grew, and finally discuss the relationship you now have with the Father through the Spirit.

These three parts will guide us in the process of transformation.

•**First leg:** We must receive. To embrace the life the Father has for us, He has released the Holy Spirit to indwell those who repent and turn from the things that have taken the place of God in our lives. John begins with the word "receive." It is essential to begin the process of repentance by receiving what God has for us. Receiving is about turning from our old ways to embrace a new way. When we release our past dependencies, we are able to have open hands to receive Christ and His Kingdom. When we reach to receive Christ we naturally let go of what we held on to in the past.

•**Second leg:** We believe when we receive the power of the Holy Spirit. Prior to that, we don't have the ability to conjure up life changing *pisteuo* belief on our own. As I mentioned earlier the word *pisteuo* is to be "all in." John says when we receive the Holy Spirit, we will have the power and ability to

receive life giving *pisteuo*. The word "believe" in this passage is a gift from the Spirit that empowers us to *be "all in"*. It is impossible to be all in without the power given by the Spirit.

•**Third leg:** The natural result of the first two legs leads us to become children of God. When the first two things occur, the third will follow as we enter an intimate and dependent relationship with God the Father. Each leg reinforces the others.

DANGEROUS EVANGELISTIC ASSUMPTIONS

CONVERSATIONS
Avoiding Presentations

Past evangelistic methods made some basic assumptions. Just 25 years ago, you could assume a majority of people believed in Heaven and Hell, good and evil, right and wrong.

Evangelistic models built on those assumptions won't work today.

Two of most Americans' greatest fears are discussing death and speaking with strangers. The Evangelism Explosion opening question is, "If you were to die tonight do you know where you would spend eternity?" A follow up question is, "Why should God allow you to spend eternity in Heaven?"

If Americans hate to talk with strangers or discuss death, how could that opening work today? Both questions assume that the participants believe in Heaven and Hell, and in an all powerful, eternal God. Those assumptions are no longer commonly held beliefs. We live in a secular, relativistic world. It is common to hear that "those assumptions may be good for you, but they don't apply to me." I frequently encounter individuals whose worldview is far more secular than most evangelistic training tools account for.

The practice of evangelism in America has been developed in an environment of cultural Christianity, in which almost everyone knew the basics of the Christian faith. Not too long ago, almost everyone had a quiet respect for Christian values and were favorably disposed to them. Evangelism then motivated people to act on what they already knew and, in a sense, already intellectually approved. You could assume that with a simple prompting a person would realign themselves to Christian values rather quickly. We know now that in too many cases, these individuals were merely brushing up against cultural Christianity without ever really responding to Christ.

You can no longer assume the current culture embraces biblical values. There seems actually to be a cultural resistance toward most things Christian. A recent CBS poll says 66 percent of American young adults consider Christianity as dangerous and violent as Islam.[13] Well-intentioned Christians who used ill-informed, aggressive methods to share Christ, have moved the needle of cultural opinion toward Christianity from positive to negative.

Move beyond memorized questions and pre-prescribed boilerplate conversations. Our world is too diverse for those methods to work. Feeling they must memorize an evangelism approach created a sense of dread in many Christ followers. Many admit that they don't feel competent or confident enough to even begin a spiritual conversation.

Fear of sharing our faith opened the door for a proliferation of gimmicks and evangelistic fads. Though created with good motives, they have an unintended negative effect. Instead of sharing life and engaging a lost world with the life changing power of Christ, we come off as high-pressure salesmen who nervously share a spiritual message to which we're marginally committed.

Perhaps you remember some of the cycles of gimmicks used to lure potential converts into "praying the prayer."

---

[13]Foxnews.com Feburary 10, 2017

THE EVANGELISM TRACT ERA

This systematized plan armed church members with provocative booklets to place in public places. People used them for cold call presentations. Some tracts presented a set of spiritual laws or an orderly plan of how to pray a "sinner's prayer." While many people came to Christ with this approach, that method is no longer effective.

THE EVANGECUBE

This was a memory tool that helped unsure Christian propagandists launch an evangelism presentation. Of course, it was a canned approach that did not engage anyone in a spiritual conversation. The goal was to have a person unfold the critical elements of the Gospel message to an unconverted person. It was believed that the missing part of evangelism was gospel information.

But the Gospel is best communicated by a changed life, not the cerebral elements of salvation information. Intellectual facts are not all that persuasive.

THE GOSPEL BLIMP

Then there was the "Gospel Blimp." A group of sincere but misguided church folks decided to reach their beer drinking, non-church attending neighbors by renting a blimp. At first they advertise their church from the blimp. When that didn't work they decided to drop propaganda leaflets from the blimp onto their neighbors. When that didn't work, they took the radical approach of just getting to know their neighbors. The final approach obviously had much better results. Christians who relate are more approachable and less disputatious.

Most of the actions are loaded with the expectation that an act of kindness will soften the recipient so they will "make a decision" to become a Christian.

To the extent that any of these approaches introduced people to Christ I am genuinely grateful. Each of these gimmicks had some effectiveness in their eras. When the gimmick becomes the focus instead of the conversation, results almost always evaporate.

None of the gimmick cycles lasted for any significant length of time. Many of us had some of those gimmicks tried on us. If you are like me you want to pull the person aside and give them a few pointers, like, "Why don't you just try to have a conversation instead of ramming some strange tool in their face?"

The days of effective evangelism gimmicks are over. Our culture has become so resistant to anything that looks or smells like propaganda that people abruptly cut the presentation off after the opening sentence. The relational approach is our most effective tool in our post Christian culture -- learn to listen to and cooperate with the Holy Spirit to find receptive, disciple-able people .

Obviously spiritual conversations are more than gimmicks. Anything that engages a person in a conversation will be of help. The goal must be to look for encounters to build bridges, which lead to transformation of one person at a time. Life change cannot be mass produced. The 1960's and 70's saw the era of "mass evangelism" but that's a misnomer. Life change that resulted from the success of crusades and large public Christian events really was the result of crucial conversations.

Research by the Billy Graham Evangelistic Association discovered that most individuals who responded at their crusades came with a friend who had been investing in them. There had been a series of crucial conversations leading up to the person's response at the "mass evangelism" event.

When I do training events, I often ask for a show of hands to see how many Christ-followers came to faith by making one big decision at a public Christian event. Among young adults usually only one or two raise their hands. Research done by Vision New England indicates that nearly nine out of ten new Christ followers described their faith as a "process." Our relational interactions inform the process that leads to transformation. There is strong evidence here that God wants to use ordinary Christians to advance His kingdom, one conversation at a time.[14]

Learning to develop an ear, fine-tuned to the promptings of the Holy Spirit, takes some practice and coaching. Most of us are not very good at listening to the gentle leading of the Holy Spirit. This skill will be the center piece of any effective crucial conversation.

---

[14] Pollock, Doug. God Space.Group Publishing, Loveland Co 2009 p 95.

BRAIN TWEAK
Stories vs Evangelism

When you read scripture stories you don't see any disciples having what we would call an "evangelistic presentation." There are countless accounts of regular people simply sharing their story of how Jesus changed their life. They did not necessarily quote scriptures. They just shared their story. For many Christians this requires a brain tweak. I recommend that we learn how to graciously connect our story to the person we are talking to. This will require some training and the direction of the Holy Spirit.

THE TWO BUCKET ICON

TOOL BOX
Two bucket Icon

At the last second, a couple glided into the open spot in line to join me on the ski lift. They both had warm smiles and seemed friendly enough. We exchanged nods and lowered the lap bar. They clicked on their tunes and zoned out. About two minutes into the ride, the lift jerked hard and suddenly stopped. We unplugged our headphones and started talking about the potential for a long delay. Before long, we were immersed in a full-blown conversation.

It appeared they were from India and were probably Hindu. I asked if they were from the southern part of the country. They lit up and asked me how I had guessed correctly. I told them I had spent some time there and as they spoke, I noticed things that seemed familiar to the region. It turned out, I had spent time in their very city. This opened up an entire new level of conversation. They seemed excited to talk with someone who knew about their home.

The Holy Spirit was nudging me to carefully follow Him into this conversation. In the very short time I had been with this couple, my heart had expanded toward them. I had no idea where this conversation was headed, but I quietly hoped I'd be able to be a part of their spiritual journey.

I told them, "When I went to India I didn't know what to expect. I was surprised at how God gave me a love for the people there in a very short time."

They asked me, "Why do you think that is?" This was my chance. I had to be careful not to try to trounce on a small spark of interest.

"There was a time when I didn't have much interest in anyone but myself," I said. "I had little tolerance or patience for people who were different from me. I had a spiritual encounter with Jesus that changed my life."

They both just sat there for a moment. I wasn't sure how this was landing. Had I over shared? Had I rushed in too soon? Was I listening well enough to the lead of the Spirit? Their silence was killing me. It was probably only four seconds, but it felt like an hour.

Then one of them said, "Yeah, I have heard people talk like that about Jesus. We worship Jesus, but I don't know much about Him, really."

I asked him to tell me more about what he knew of Jesus since he was raised Hindu. He gave a sterile, historic answer. I asked him, "Where do you land on this topic?" I wondered if I had been too forceful when he paused again. Oh no, I thought, not another hour-long pause.

After a few seconds, he said, "I am intrigued about why you keep speaking of Jesus in such a personal way." I asked him to picture life as organized in several buckets. One of them is for relationships, another is for religious events. For me Jesus was in the bucket of personal relationships. He is as personal as anyone in my life.

I explained that when I started my spiritual search a few years ago, I was surprised to find Jesus was not about the religion bucket. He paused again.

For me religion has always been its own bucket. Religion and relationships are completely different.

He said, "I don't understand why you talk like you do." I explained that I am not a very religious person. I don't do much in the way of religion. I had a time in my life when someone introduced me to Jesus. They didn't just show me the historical information from the Bible. They spoke like I do about Jesus in a relational way. I had never heard someone talk like that. I had to know more. They introduced me to Him like you would a friend. I later realized that this can happen because Jesus is not a dead historical figure. He is alive and wants to live with you in a spiritual way.

He shook his head, and said he was fascinated and would love to know more. "This is like nothing I have ever known before," he said. His religion and relationship buckets were always separate.

Just about that time, the lift jerked and we began to move. I knew we had about two minutes to wrap up this conversation. I suggested they could prayerfully talk directly to Jesus and that God would help them to communicate. I told them I believed they would be pleasantly surprised at the results. By this time, we were ready to off load from the lift. We said how much we enjoyed meeting and talking together. Since we lived about 10 miles apart, I gave them my card and suggested that we get together for coffee when we returned. We said goodbye and parted.

It was a conversation that gave me a chance to use the "Two Bucket Icon" even though I couldn't draw it out. When I have the chance to draw the images, I discuss how most of us relate to religion and relationships very differently. They are not in the same category. Following Jesus is in the relational bucket, not the religious. This distinction will create an entire series of conversations that re-categorize what it means to follow Jesus.

Those who assume Jesus belongs in the religious bucket think He is about religious events, moralism, and behavior modification, someone who makes us "Heaven eligible." I was able to use my Christ-encounter story in a way that opened a spiritual conversation.

This couple was not afraid to discuss spiritual things. The Holy Spirit put me in the right place at the right time. I thanked God for arranging our meeting. I continued to pray that the couple would follow the promptings of the Spirit. Learning to follow promptings of the Holy Spirit and learning to share my "Christ encounter story" were integral to the spiritual conversation that developed that day.

PRESSURE TO HAVE A DRAMATIC CONVERSION STORY

I have a dramatic conversion story. I died in surgery and had an "out of body experience." I seldom share those dramatic elements because I don't want the focus to be on my hospital experience. I want people to know how transforming a relationship with Jesus can be.

Too many Christians feel they can't share their story because it is not interesting enough. The opposite is true. The most powerful story is always the retelling of what Jesus has done in a life. Dramatic testimonies can actually demotivate people who feel their story isn't riveting enough. The average Christ follower doesn't have a radical conversion experience. The non-dramatic story is in many ways the more powerful because it is the more common experience.

Most stories can be entertaining if we learn how to tell them. The average Christian feels that their story is boring. The more sensational the story, the harder it is for the average person to relate. The result can be entertainment without spiritual impact. Your goal is not to impress them with a sensational story, but to follow the Holy Spirit's lead and allow Him to impact their lives. Remember, the Father will use your story. If you don't have a dramatic conversion event story, you are probably more like the average person.

JESUS SHARED STORIES,
NOT EVANGELISTIC PRESENTATIONS

Jesus used stories from real life. He did not share unnecessary details. He described common things to help people better understand how His new kingdom worked. He shared a story of how a father dealt with two sons, one was obedient and the other disobedient. He extracted a principle of grace from how a business owner treated laborers he had hired at intervals throughout the day.

Jesus opened people's eyes with His insightful stories. He compared soils to teach us that our hearts need to be properly prepared. He taught about eternity by using the rich man's eye-of-the-needle comparison. He cautioned us that we are accountable for how we live our lives by the lessons of the unproductive fig tree. His stories all revealed the heart of the Father for us.

THE FIVE QUALITIES OF JESUS'
CRUCIAL CONVERSATIONS

1. JESUS ENGAGED ORDINARY PEOPLE IN CRUCIAL CONVERSATIONS.

The people who became followers of Jesus in the Gospel accounts were comprised simply of the people who were at hand. These people were available. This reminds us that there are disciple-able people in every culture and community.

2. JESUS STARTED WITH PEOPLE WHO WERE SPIRITUALLY OPEN.

Jesus didn't spend time recruiting people within the temple. For example, he called fishermen who were minding their own business, focusing on earning their living. They didn't have to believe already that Jesus was the Son of God or to trust some theological statement. They just had to be willing to follow Him.

3. CRUCIAL CONVERSATIONS WERE THE CONSTANT CONTEXT FOR ALL JESUS DID.

Jesus went to parties, weddings, and people's homes for dinner. People introduced him to their friends. In this way Jesus became involved in natural networks of relationships:

> *"While Jesus was having dinner at Levi's house, many tax collectors and sinners were eating with him and his disciples, for there were many who followed him. "*
> - Mark 2:15

4. JESUS' CONVERSATIONS WERE PRACTICAL, NOT INTELLECTUAL.

Jesus based most of his conversations on spontaneous life situations. He used everyday illustrations people could understand

5. JESUS STARTED WHERE THE PERSON WAS, AND PROCEEDED FROM THERE.

Jesus allowed the person with whom He was talking to direct the course of the conversation. Whether it was a rich, young, intellectual, a social outcast, demoniac, or a religious leader, they set the conversation. They brought the topic to Jesus, He didn't begin with a canned presentation.

Crucial Questions

Crucial Questions
For Bridge Building

Crucial questions
knowing God

•Why do you think so many people try so hard to live good lives?

•Where do you think we get that drive?

•Have you noticed that many people choose to live as if God does not exist? Why do you think that happens?

•What should God do to validate His existence and bring you to belief?

Crucial Questions
that make you think about God

•What do you hope is true about God?

•Some people believe we are the product of a random evolutionary process. What do you think?

•Has your belief or disbelief in God affected your life?

•What is the big question that you can't wait to ask God?

crucial

CHANGING

HOW WE DISCIPLE

conversations

SECTION 6

SPIRITUAL   GAP

Jesus' First Disciple - John The Baptizer
John 1:6-13 & John 3:16-18 & John 10:41-42

John 1:6-8 There was a man sent from God whose name was John. He came as a witness to testify concerning that light, so that through him all might believe. He himself was not the light; he came only as a witness to the light.

John 1:12-13 Yet to all who did receive him, to those who believed in his name, he gave the right to become children of God— children born not of natural descent, nor of human decision or a husband's will, but born of God.

John 3:16 For God so loved the world that he gave his one and only Son, that whoever *pisteuo*/believed in him shall not perish but have eternal life.

John 3:17 For God did not send his Son into the world to condemn the world, but to save the world through him.

John 3:18 Whoever pisteuo/believes in him is not condemned, but whoever does not pisteuo/believe stands condemned already because they have not pisteuo/believed in the name of God's one and only Son.

John 10:41-42 Many people...said, "Though John never performed a sign, all that John said about this man Jesus was true." And many pisteuo/believed in Jesus.

" A true disciple is a disciple maker."
-Francis Chan

"You can't fulfill God's purpose for your life while focusing
on your own plans."
-Rick Warren

CHAPTER 12

CRUCIAL CONVERSATIONS WITH JESUS' FIRST DISCIPLE

Apparently the freight train of God's glory and grace collided with the slow moving vehicle of John the Baptist's life. We don't know much about how it happened. All we know is the evidence that John was a changed man. He was transformed by spending time with Jesus and from the influence of the Essene community of disciples.

The Essenes spent their lives preparing the way for the Messiah to launch His Kingdom movement. Yet Jesus didn't make John one of the twelve. John was beheaded early in the movement and didn't get the opportunity to engage in any of the miraculous events like the other disciples. John 10:41-42 says;

> *"They said, 'Though John never performed a sign, all that John said about this man Jesus was true.' And many* **believed/pisteuo** *in Jesus." (because of John.)*

In the short period when John spoke about the impact of Jesus on his life, many people stepped across the line of faith/pisteuo to trust Jesus. That is my prayer for my time here on space ship earth. I want to use my time here to have crucial conversations that change people's eternity.

CONVERSATIONS
John and Jesus

Jesus tapped John to launch the movement that changed the world. Jesus' baptism and crucifixion are the only two events of Jesus' life mentioned in all four Gospels. Jesus chose to go public with His baptism just outside of Jerusalem, immediately after a festival. Throngs of pilgrims are taking the trade route along the Jordan river north.

The baptism story is so prominent because it is the genesis of the movement that you have embraced two thousand years later. This movement has changed our lives for all eternity.

BRAIN TWEAK
Jesus's First Disciple

I have asked hundreds of pastors, **"Who was Jesus' first disciple?"** I seldom get the answer, "John the Baptist." In scripture, it is clear in whom Jesus first invested time and energy. The Apostle John records the conversation between Jesus and "John the Baptizer" in John 1:26-27:

> *"Among you stands one you do not know... the straps of whose sandals I am not worthy to untie."*

Jesus apparently had begun to cultivate His first disciple long before anyone began to record the events in His life. That could explain why there is no record of His training of John, even though John is His first established associate. It would be naive to think that one day at age 30 the Father suddenly opened the breaker panel and flipped the Messiah switch on for Jesus.

We know some of the backstory between Jesus and John. We know about the angelic updates prior to both of their births. From the beginning, Jesus and John were part of a bigger picture in which they were more than cousins. Interestingly, their lives took very different paths of preparation for the launching of this new Kingdom. Yet their intertwined paths meet in adulthood and now the Kingdom rocket has liftoff.

John introduced Jesus to his circle of relationships. John had methodically discipled a group of men. We don't know how John trained and empowered this group to prepare the way for the Messiah. In the first chapter of John, we see John the Baptist releasing a group of his followers to attach themselves to Jesus. This group would be half of the original twelve disciples. They would become the movement makers in the Kingdom that Jesus was launching. John introduced Jesus to three pairs of men. The first were Andrew and Peter, the next were Phillip and Nathaniel, and then James and John. Jesus takes these men and combines them with six others He has prepared. He trains them to have crucial kingdom conversations. He would commission these men to take the movement to the next level.

John releases his life work into the hands of the Messiah. John's followers will become the building blocks for Jesus. Jesus didn't just simply invite the six to become His inner core on this first encounter. Initially, Jesus offers a simple two-word invitation: "follow me." This is the most simple of tests. If this group is willing to embrace the challenges offered by Jesus to "follow" then they would be invited to the next step of becoming a part of the twelve. Mark 3:13-14 says:

> *"Jesus went up on a mountainside and called to him those (disciples) he wanted, and they came to him. He appointed twelve that they might be with him and that he might send them out."*

This select group spent time simply watching and listening to Jesus' conversations. They were from every strata of culture and from a variety of socio-economic levels.

THE ETERNAL PERSPECTIVE MOTIVATES CRUCIAL CONVERSATIONS

John had a great perspective on living for eternity. He knew that time was short. He couldn't have known how short. He was executed in the opening months of the movement. But he had a huge impact in a very short time. The gospels open with this phrase from John 1:6-8:

> *"There was a man sent from God whose name was John. He came as a witness to testify concerning that light, so that through him all might believe/pisteuo."*

John lived like he knew his time was brief, and every moment mattered. That explains his intense personality. John held on to this world loosely. He viewed everything with eternal lenses. He had a voracious passion to connect with others. His heart seemed to break for those who had been rejected by the religious establishment.

John knew that people who feel condemned and rejected run from the Father, the very One who longs to heal and restore them. The Apostle John says in John 1:10:

> *" (Jesus) was in the world, and though the world was made through him, the world did not recognize him…"*

John the Baptist's conversations point to our need for Jesus and how we can view this temporal work correctly. Living with an eternal perspective requires an intentional way of viewing the world.

EXAMPLES
Living For Eternity

I was sitting in a meeting recently when the leader began to roll out all the things he had purchased that day. He bought new king size sheets and a comforter, a super large flat screen TV, and new bath towels. No one seemed surprised by his purchases until he announced that they were all for his hotel room down the street from where we were meeting. The ordinary purchases suddenly took on new meaning.

No one goes to that trouble and expense for a temporary hotel accommodation. Then he reminded us of how we do the very same thing. Do we believe that our lives here are but a brief temporal passing to our forever eternal home? If we believe this is not our home, why do we invest everything like this is our final destination?

He had us. We were all guilty of trying to supersize our temporary hotel room. In so doing, we become distracted from the more eternal mission. He walked across the front of the room and began to put a sticker that said "on-loan" on a dollhouse, on a toy car, and on a dollhouse-sized office cubicle that represented our work lives.

"If you are living for these things, you are living a life of brief pleasure, short lived satisfaction, and temporary fulfillment," he said. Everything in our lives is on-loan.

"There is only *one* thing in our lives that is not temporary," he continued. "There is only one thing you can take with you into the next world. When you breathe your last breath you want your life to have been about eternal things. When we overly invest in "on loan" items we are left feeling empty and hollow.

I first realized, I must view this temporary life through the lens of eternity, one day while I was on air as a radio DJ. I had just recently given my life to Christ. I was praying during one of my breaks. The control room was an isolated soundproof box with no windows. I was in the middle of an expanded news break. This 15-minute conversation with the Father was as real as any conversation I have ever had. I was reading a passage in 1 Corinthians 3:12-16. The point of this scripture is direct and clear. Everything in our lives is "on-loan" and it will soon be gone. Anyone who invests in the short term will be disappointed because nothing will last. No earthly commodity can be transferred from this world to the next; not land, homes, bank accounts, titles, or achievements.

I vividly remember praying, "Father what could I do with my life that would make an impact?" I had never thought before that the only investment I can make with my life that will have eternal significance is to invest in people. They will live eternally. Why have I spent so much energy investing in things that were not eternal? That reality gripped me. That day I made the shift to invest in people who will live forever somewhere.

From that day on, I regularly asked myself if what I'm giving my life to at the moment is eternal or temporal? Getting off track will have eternal implications. It is easy to lose our focus and begin to give our lives to pursuing possessions, security, pleasure, power, or popularity. It was clearly futile to live to collect things that were merely on loan to me for a short season.

This thought would not leave me. Jesus had invited me to join Him just like he invited John. Together they launched a movement that transcended money, power, or earthly influence. They were on a mission. Their every thought focused on what mattered most. They would engage common people in conversations that led them to reach out to the Father.

Jesus has invited you and me on the same mission. Nobody can reach your corner of the world as effectively as you can. To do this, I realized I must make some changes. I would need to learn how to have effective spiritual conversations. The single greatest gift that I could give someone is a conversation that focuses on how they can be rightly connected to the One who changes lives.

Are you willing to seize the opportunities for spiritual conversations? Have you asked Him to give you a tender open heart, and a passion for the people the Father is leading your way?

From this point on, your goal is to take every opportunity to try to identify those who are searching for direction and answers. I believe the Father regularly puts spiritual searchers in your path.

Will you be prepared to take the next step? Someone took an interest in your spiritual welfare. They probably cared enough to engage you in a conversation, and they had an influence in your spiritual development. If you really think through your faith journey, I'll bet you can quickly identify a Christ-follower who got involved and they took the time to show you love and compassion.

The message only advances when it is transmitted from one life to another life. It doesn't spread through institutional methods. You and I must become contagious. We must sneeze the message of Jesus forward. People don't catch life transformation from institutions or programs.

When you caught this Jesus thing, I'll bet you immediately began to live differently. You probably began to extend yourself, and care for people you otherwise would not have reached out to. When Jesus takes up residence in us we can't help but respond differently to the world around us. That is how you and I know of Jesus on a continent half way around the world from where this originated 2,000 years ago.

I can point to that day in the control booth as a turning point in my life. I began to live more intentionally toward eternity from that day forward.

At some point, if you are a follower of Jesus, you are going to breath your last lung full of air on this planet. When you exhale that final time, and step into eternity you will meet all of the people who have been described in this book. There will be Natalie, standing beside Nicodemus, and Aban standing with John the Baptizer. We will have a collective appreciation for those who took the time to have a crucial conversation with us. I don't know about you, but I can't think of a more important thing we can do as long as we are in these earth suits.

Keep having crucial conversations until Jesus returns!

CRUCIAL QUESTIONS

CRUCIAL QUESTIONS
For Bridge Building

CRUCIAL QUESTIONS
CONSIDERING THE BIG PICTURE

• If you only had six months to live, what would be on your list of things to do before you die?

• What causes you to be hopeful about your future?

• What scares you the most about letting God alter your life?

CRUCIAL QUESTIONS
RELATIVE TRUTH

• It sounds as if you value open-mindedness. Do you ever find yourself closing your mind to certain things, ideas, or people?

• What criteria do you use to determine whether something is true?

• Does your worldview allow for any absolutes?

crucial

CRUCIAL

CONVERSATIONS

APPENDIX A

conversations

223 QUESTIONS JESUS ASKED

223 QUESTIONS
JESUS ASKED

1. And if you greet your brethren only, what is unusual about that… unbelievers do the same? (Matt 5:47)

2. Can any of you by worrying add a single moment to your lifespan? (Matt 6:27)

3. Why are you anxious about clothes? (Matt 6:28)

4. Why do you notice the splinter in your brother's eye yet fail to perceive the wooden beam in your own eye? (Matt 7:3)

5. Do people pick grapes from thorn bushes or figs from thistles? (Matt 7:16)

6. Why are you terrified? (Matt 8:26)

7. Why do you harbor evil thoughts? (Matt 9:4)

8. Can the wedding guests mourn so long as the Bridegroom is with them? (Matt 9:15)

9. Do you believe I can do this? (Matt 9:28)

10. What did you go out to the desert to see? (Matt 11:8)

11. To what shall I compare this generation? (Matt 11:6)

12. Which of you who has a sheep that falls into a pit on the Sabbath will not take hold of it and lift it out? (Matt 12:11)

13. How can anyone enter a strong man's house and take hold of his possessions unless he first ties up the strong man? (Matt 12:29)

14. You brood of vipers! How can you say good things when you are evil? (Matt 12:34)

15. Who is my mother? Who are my brothers? (Matt 12:48)

16. Why did you doubt? (Matt 14:31)

17. And why do you break the commandments of God for the sake of your tradition? (Matt 15:3)

18. How many loaves do you have? (Matt 15:34)

19. Do you not yet understand? (Matt 16:8)

20. Who do people say the Son of Man is? (Matt 16:13)

21. But who do you say that I am? (Matt 16:15)

22. What profit would there be for one to gain the whole world and forfeit his soul and what can one give in exchange for his life? (Matt 16:26)

23. O faithless and perverse generation how long must I endure you? (Matt 17:17)

24. Why do you ask me about what is good? (Matt 19:16)

25. Can you drink the cup that I am going to drink? (Matt 20:22)

26. What do you want me to do for you? (Matt 20:32)

27. Did you never read the scriptures? (Matt 21:42)

28. Why are you testing me? (Matt 22:18)

29. Blind fools, which is greater, the gold or the temple that makes the gold sacred....the gift of the altar that makes the gift sacred? (Matt 23:17-19)

30. How are you to avoid being sentenced to hell? (Matt 23:33)

31. Why do you make trouble for the woman? (Matt 26:10)

32. Could you not watch for me one brief hour? (Matt 26:40)

33. Do you think I cannot call upon my Father and he will not provide me at this moment with more than 12 legions of angels? (Matt 26:53)

34. Have you come out as against a robber with swords and clubs to seize me? (Matt 26:55)

35. My God, My God, Why have you forsaken me? (Matt 27:46)

36. Why are you thinking such things in your heart? (Mark 2:8)

37. Is a lamp brought to be put under a basket or under a bed rather than on a lamp stand? (Mark 4:21)

38. Who has touched my clothes? (Mark 5:30)

39. Why this commotion and weeping? (Mark 5:39)

40. Are even you likewise without understanding? (Mark 7:18)

41. Why does this generation seek a sign? (Mark 8:12)

42. Do you not yet understand or comprehend? Are your hearts hardened? Do you have eyes and still not see? Ears and not hear? (Mark 8:17-18)

43. How many wicker baskets full of leftover fragments did you pick up? (Mark 8:19)

44. What were you arguing about on the way? (Mark 9:33)

45. Salt is good, but what if salt becomes flat? (Mark 9:50)

46. What did Moses command you? (Mark 10:3)

47. Do you see these great buildings? They will all be thrown down. (Mark 13:2)

48. Simon, are you asleep? (Mark 14:37)

49. Why were you looking for me? (Luke 2:49)

50. What are you thinking in your hearts? (Luke 5:22)

51. Why do you call me 'Lord, Lord' and not do what I command? (Luke 6:46)

52. Where is your faith (Luke 8:25)

53. What is your name? (Luke 8:30)

54. Who touched me? (Luke 8:45)

55. Will you be exalted to heaven? (Luke 10:15)

56. What is written in the law? How do you read it? (Luke 10:26)

57. Which of these three in your opinion was neighbor to the robber's victim? (Luke 10:36)

58. Did not the maker of the outside also make the inside? (Luke 11:40)

59. Friend, who appointed me as your judge and arbiter? (Luke 12:14)

60. If even the smallest things are beyond your control, why are you anxious about the rest? (Luke 12:26)

61. Why do you not judge for yourself what is right? (Luke 12:57)

62. What king, marching into battle would not first sit down and decide whether with ten thousand troops he can successfully oppose another king marching upon him with twenty thousand troops? (Luke 14:31)

63. If therefore you are not trustworthy with worldly wealth, who will trust you with true wealth? (Luke 16:11)

64. Has none but this foreigner returned to give thanks to God? (Luke 17:18)

65. Will not God then secure the rights of his chosen ones who call out to him day and night? (Luke 18:7)

66. But when the Son of Man comes, will he find any faith on earth? (Luke 18:8)

67. For who is greater, the one seated at the table or the one who serves? (Luke 22:27)

68. Why are you sleeping? (Luke 22:46)

69. For if these things are done when the wood is green, what will happen when it is dry? (Luke 23:31)

70. What are you discussing as you walk along? (Luke 24:17)

71. Was it not necessary that the Messiah should suffer these things and then enter his glory? (Luke 24:26)

72. Have you anything here to eat? (Luke 24:41)

73. What are you looking for? (John 1:38)

74. Why do you involve me? (John 2:4)

75. You are a teacher in Israel and you do not understand this? (John 3: 10)

76. If I tell you about earthly things and you will not believe, how will you believe when I tell you of heavenly things? (John 3: 12)

77. Do you want to be well? (John 5:6)

78. How is it that you seek praise from one another and not seek the praise that comes from God? (John 5:44)

79. If you do not believe Moses' writings how will you believe me? (John 5:47)

80. Where can we buy enough food for them to eat? (John 6:5)

81. Does this (teaching of the Eucharist) shock you? (John 6:61)

82. Do you also want to leave me? (John 6:67)

83. Why are you trying to kill me? (John 7:19)

84. Woman where are they, has no one condemned you? (John 8:10)

85. Why do you not understand what I am saying? (John 8:43)

86. Can any of you charge me with sin? (John 8:46)

87. If I am telling you the truth, why do you not believe me? (John 8:46)

88. Are there not twelve hours in a day? (John 11:9)

89. Do you believe this? (John 11:26)

90. Do you realize what I have done for you? (John 13:12)

91. Have I been with you for so long and still you do not know me? (John 14:9)

92. Whom are you looking for? (John 18:4)

93. Shall I not drink the cup the Father gave me? (John 18:11)

94. If I have spoken rightly, why did you strike me? (John 18:23)

95. Do you say [what you say about me] on your own or have others been telling you about me? (John 18:34)

96. Have you come to believe because you have seen me? (John 20:29)

97. Do you love me? (John 21:16)

98. What if I want John to remain until I come? (John 21:22)

99. What concern is it of yours? (John 21:22)

100. If you love those who love you, what reward will you get? (Matthew 5:46)

101. Which is easier: to say, 'Your sins are forgiven,' or to say, 'Get up and walk'? (Matthew 9:5)

102. Do you believe that I am able to do this? (Matthew 9:28)

103. If any of you has a sheep and it falls into a pit on the Sabbath, will you not take hold of it and lift it out? (Matthew 12:11)

104. How can anyone enter a strong man's house and carry off his possessions unless he first ties up the strong man? (Matthew 12:29)

105. You brood of vipers, how can you who are evil say anything good? (Matthew 12:34)

106. Who is my mother, and who are my brothers? (Matthew 12:48)

107. Why did you doubt? (Matthew 14:31)

108. Why do you break the command of God for the sake of your tradition? (Matthew 15:3)

109. How many loaves do you have? (Matthew 15:34)

110. Do you still not understand? (Matthew 16:9)

111. Who do people say the Son of Man is? (Matthew 16:13)

112. Who do you say I am? (Matthew 16:15)

113. What good will it be for a man if he gains the whole world, yet forfeits his soul? Or what can a man give in exchange for his soul? (Matthew 16:26)

114. How long shall I stay with you? How long shall I put up with you? (Matthew 17:17)

115. From whom do the kings of the earth collect duty and taxes–from their own sons or from others? (Matthew 17:25)

116. What do you think? If a man owns a hundred sheep, and one of them wanders away, will he not leave the ninety-nine on the hills and go to look for the one that wandered off? (Matthew 18:12)

117. Why do you ask me about what is good? (Matthew 19:17)

118. What is it you want? (Matthew 20:21)

119. Can you drink the cup I am going to drink? (Matthew 20:22)

120. What do you want me to do for you? (Matthew 20:32)

121. John's baptism—where did it come from? Was it from heaven, or from men? (Matthew 21:25)

122. What do you think? (Matthew 21:28)

123. Have you never read in the Scriptures? (Matthew 21:42)

124. Why are you trying to trap me? (Matthew 22:18)

125. What do you think about the Christ? Whose son is he? (Matthew 22:42)

126. Which is greater: the gold, or the temple that makes the gold sacred? Which is greater: the gift, or the altar that makes the gift sacred? (Matthew 23:17-19)

127. How will you escape being condemned to hell? (Matthew 23:33)

128. Why are you bothering this woman? (Matthew 26:10)

129. Could you men not keep watch with me for one hour? (Matthew 26:40)

130. Do you think I cannot call on my Father, and he will at once put at my disposal more than twelve legions of angels? (Matthew 26:53)

131. But how then would the Scriptures be fulfilled that say it must happen in this way? (Matthew 26:54)

132. Am I leading a rebellion, that you have come out with swords and clubs to capture me? (Matthew 26:55)My God, my God, why have you forsaken me? (Matthew 27:46)

133. Why are you thinking these things? (Mark 2:8)

134. Do you bring in a lamp to put it under a bowl or a bed? Instead, don't you put it on its stand? (Mark 4:21)

135. What shall we say the kingdom of God is like, or what parable shall we use to describe it? (Mark 4:30)

136. Why are you so afraid? Do you still have no faith? (Mark 4:40)

137. What is your name? (Mark 5:9)

138. Who touched my clothes? (Mark 5:30)

139. Why all this commotion and wailing? (Mark 5:39)

140. Are you so dull? (Mark 7:18)

141. Don't you see that nothing that enters a man from the outside can make him 'unclean'? (Mark 7:18)

142. Why does this generation ask for a miraculous sign? I tell you the truth, no sign will be given to it. (Mark 8:12)

143. Why are you talking about having no bread? Do you still not see or understand? Are your hearts hardened? Do you have eyes but fail to see, and ears but fail to hear? And don't you remember? (Mark 8:17-18)

144. When I broke the five loaves for the five thousand, how many basketfuls of pieces did you pick up? (Mark 8:19)

145. When I broke the seven loaves for the four thousand, how many basketfuls of pieces did you pick up? (Mark 8:20)

146. Do you still not understand? (Mark 8:21)

147. [To the blind man] Do you see anything? (Mark 8:23)

148. Why then is it written that the Son of Man must suffer much and be rejected? (Mark 9:12)

149. What were you arguing about on the road? (Mark 9:33)

150. Salt is good, but if it loses its saltiness, how can you make it salty again? (Mark 9:50)

151. What did Moses command you? (Mark 10:3)

152. Why do you call me good? (Mark 10:18)

153. What do you want me to do for you? (Mark 10:51)

154. Why are you trying to trap me? (Mark 12:15)

155. Do you see all these great buildings? (Mark 13:2)

156. Are you asleep? (Mark 14:37)

157. Could you not keep watch for one hour? (Mark 14:37)

158. Why were you searching for me? (Luke 2:49)

159. Didn't you know I had to be in my Father's house? (Luke 2:49)

160. Why are you thinking these things in your hearts? (Luke 5:22)

161. Which is easier: to say, 'Your sins are forgiven,' or to say, 'Get up and walk'? (Luke 5:23)

162. Why do you call me, 'Lord, Lord,' and do not do what I say? (Lk 6:46)

163. Where is your faith? (Luke 8:25)

164. What is your name? (Luke 8:30)

165. Who touched me? (Luke 8:45)

166. Will you be lifted up to the skies? (Luke 10:15)

167. What is written in the Law? How do you read it? (Luke 10:26)

168. Which of these three do you think was a neighbor to the man who fell into the hands of robbers? (Luke 10:36)

169. Did not the one who made the outside make the inside also? (Luke 11:40)

170. Who appointed me a judge or an arbiter between you? (Luke 12:14-15)

171. Who of you by worrying can add a single hour to his life? (Luke 12:25)

172. Why don't you judge for yourselves what is right? (Luke 12:57)

173. Or suppose a king is about to go to war against another king. Will he not first sit down and consider whether he is able with ten thousand men to oppose the one coming against him with twenty thousand? (Luke 14:31)

174. Salt is good, but if it loses its saltiness, how can it be made salty again? (Luke 14:34)

175. Suppose one of you has a hundred sheep and loses one of them. Does he not leave the ninety-nine in the open country and go after the lost sheep until he finds it? (Luke 15:4)

176. Or suppose a woman has ten silver coins and loses one. Does she not light a lamp, sweep the house and search carefully until she finds it? (Luke 15:8)

177. So if you have not been trustworthy in handling worldly wealth, who will trust you with true riches? (Luke 16:11)

178. Were not all ten cleansed? Where are the other nine? (Luke 17:17)

179. And will not God bring about justice for his chosen ones, who cry out to him day and night? Will he keep putting them off? (Luke 18:7)

180. However, when the Son of Man comes, will he find faith on the earth? (Luke 18:8)

181. For who is greater, the one who is at the table or the one who serves? (Luke 22:27)

182. Why are you sleeping? (Luke 22:46)

183. For if men do these things when the tree is green, what will happen when it is dry? (Luke 23:31)

184. What are you discussing together as you walk along? (Luke 24:17)

185. What things? (Luke 24:19)

186. Did not the Christ have to suffer these things and then enter his glory? (Luke 24:26)

187. Why are you troubled, and why do doubts rise in your minds? (Luke 24:38)

188. Do you have anything here to eat? (Luke 24:41)

189. What do you want? (John 1:38)

190. Why do you involve me? (John 2:4)

191. You are Israel's teacher, and do you not understand? (John 3:10)

192. I have spoken to you of earthly things and you do not believe; how then will you believe if I speak of heavenly things? (John 3:12)

193. Will you give me a drink? (John 4:7)

194. Do you want to get well? (John 5:6)

195. How can you believe if you accept praise from one another, yet make no effort to obtain the praise that comes from the only God? (John 5:44)

196. If you do not believe Moses' writings how will you believe? (John 5:47)

197. Where shall we buy bread for these people to eat? (John 6:5)

198. Does this offend you? (John 6:61)

199. What if the Son of Man ascends to where he was before! (John 6:62)

200. You do not want to leave too, do you? (John 6:67)

201. Have I not chosen you? (John 6:70)

202. Has not Moses given you the law? (John 7:19)

203. Why are you trying to kill me? (John 7:19)

204. Why are you angry with me for healing the whole man on the Sabbath? (John 7:23)

205. Where are they? Has no one condemned you? (John 8:10)

206. Why is my language not clear to you? (John 8:43)

207. Can any of you prove me guilty of sin? (John 8:46)

208. If I am telling the truth, why don't you believe me? (John 8:46)

209. Why then do you accuse me of blasphemy because I said, 'I am God's Son'? (John 10:36)

210. Are there not twelve hours of daylight? (John 11:9)

211. Do you believe this? (John 11:26)

212. Where have you laid him? (John 11:33)

213. Do you understand what I have done for you? (John 13:12)

214. Don't you know me, even after I have been among you such a long time? (John 14:9)

215. Who is it you want? (John 18:4,7)

216. Shall I not drink the cup the Father has given me? (John 18:11)

217. Is that your own idea, or did others talk to you about me? (John 18:34)

218. Why question me? (John 18:21)

219. If I spoke the truth, why did you strike me? (John 18:23)

220. Why are you crying? Who is it you are looking for? (John 20:15)

221. Friends, haven't you any fish? (John 21:5)

222. Do you love me? (John 21:17)

223. What is that to you? (John 21:22)

About The Author

Dan Grider is the founder of the Ignite Network, a nation wide network of new churches lead by millennial pastors who are launching starfish movements.

Dan is also the founding pastor of Daybreak Church and the Daybreak Network of churches in San Diego California. Dan has planted churches and pastored on both U.S. coasts.

Dan has written five books and co-authored the best selling book "The God Questions."

Follow Dan and the discipleship conversation at **IgniteDiscipleship.com**

Crucial Conversations, is also available in cases at **IgniteDiscipleship.com**

The Starfish Movement

Is available for **$10 each**
Plus $3 shipping and handling per book

Order at
IgniteDiscipleship.com
or send payment to
Po Box 70632
Knoxville, TN 37938

Jesus birthed a movement that was designed to include, engage, and inspire. However, somewhere along the way, Christian leaders began imitating the leaders who went before them instead of imitating Jesus. They became immeshed in church programs and issues of Christian sub-culture. As a result, most never experienced the power of the unstoppable mission of Jesus.

Instead, what if we were trained and empowered to become a part of that mission? What if we realized that Jesus had us in mind and created us specifically for this all along? This book is designed to do just that. It will challenge leaders to embrace the principles of the movement Jesus launched - the Starfish Movement.

Case price **$9 each** in Cases of 10
Plus $12 Shipping and Handling per case

The God Questions

Is available for **$10 each**
Plus $3 shipping and handling per book

Order at
IgniteDiscipleship.com

The God Questions will give you the courage to engage in difficult spiritual conversations, and the confidence to believe that God is big enough to answer all of your questions.

The number one reason that Christians don't share their faith is because they feel that they are not prepared to engage in serious spiritual conversations.

Instead, what if we were trained and empowered to engage in conversations with confidence and grace. This book will prepare you to face the hard questions of our day with assurance.

Case price **$9 each** in Cases of 10
Plus $12 Shipping and Handling per case